IN FULL FLIGHT

Achieving Purpose Through Attaining and Maintaining Your Natural and Spiritual Soaring Altitude

Pastor Dr. Claudine Benjamin

IN FULL FLIGHT. Copyright @ 2025. Pastor Dr. Claudine Benjamin. All rights reserved.

For more information or to book an event, contact: inspiredtowinsouls@gmail.om

No part of this publication may be reproduced, stored in a retrieval system or transmitted in any form or by any means, electronic, mechanical, photocopying, recording or otherwise without the prior written permission of the author.

Published by:

Editor: Cleveland O. McLeish (Author C. Orville McLeish)

ISBN: 978-1-965635-33-9 (paperback)

Unless otherwise stated, all Scripture quotations are taken from the King James Version (KJV). Scripture quotations marked "KJV" are taken from the Holy Bible, King James Version (Public Domain).

Scripture quotations marked (NLT) are taken from the Holy Bible, New Living Translation, copyright © 1996, 2004, 2007 by Tyndale House Foundation. Used by permission of Tyndale House Publishers, Inc., Carol Stream, Illinois 60188. All rights reserved.

Scripture quotations marked "ESV" are from the ESV Bible® (The Holy Bible, English Standard Version®), copyright © 2001 by Crossway Bibles, a publishing ministry of Good News Publishers. Used by permission. All rights reserved.

ABOUT THE AUTHOR

Pastor Claudine Benjamin is a passionate preacher, teacher, and writer with a heart for empowering individuals to rise to their God-ordained purpose. With years of pastoral ministry experience and a powerful personal testimony of spiritual resilience, she blends biblical truth with practical insight to help others navigate life's storms and soar above adversity.

As a spiritual coach and mentor, Pastor Claudine ministers with boldness, clarity, and compassion, speaking to the soul of the reader with messages of hope, healing, and purpose. Her unique writing style weaves together vivid metaphors—like the eagle's flight—with deep scriptural truths, creating life-changing lessons that resonate far beyond the page.

She is the author of several impactful works, including How to Handle the Process After the Storm, The Urgency in Winning Souls: A Quest to Fulfill the Great Commission by Winning the Lost at Any Cost, and Broken But Not Destroyed. Her teachings challenge believers to discover their calling and maintain it with discipline, discernment, and dependence on the Holy Spirit.

Whether through the pulpit, page, or prayer room, Pastor Claudine is committed to helping others rise above limitations, embrace their spiritual identity, and live life in full flight.

DEDICATION AND ACKNOWLEDGMENTS

To every dreamer who has ever stared at the sky and wondered if you were meant for more—this book is for you.

To those who have felt the stirring of purpose deep within your spirit but were afraid to leave the ground—may these pages remind you that you were created with wings and that God has destined you to fly.

To the spiritual pioneers, trailblazers, and misunderstood visionaries who kept pressing forward even when the winds were against you—thank you for teaching the rest of us that turbulence does not mean failure, and storms do not cancel destiny.

To the weary warriors who have flown through fierce battles, weathered storms, and landed broken but not defeated—your scars are not signs of shame but symbols of strength. This book honors your journey.

To the believers who crashed somewhere along the way—whether you fell through discouragement, distraction, disobedience, or despair, know this: God has not revoked your wings. This book is for your recovery, restoration, and return to the skies.

To the next generation of eagles—the Eli's who are still discovering who they are, the Zara's who are boldly soaring in their purpose, and the Obed's who carry wisdom, experience, and strength in their wings—you are the heartbeat of this message. You remind us that flight is not just a season—it's a calling, a way of life, a posture of purpose.

To my spiritual family, mentors, and the cloud of witnesses who have spoken life into me, corrected me, prayed for me, and reminded me who I am when I forget—You helped me spread my wings.

To every pastor, prophet, leader, intercessor, worshipper, and child of God reading this—thank you for saying yes to the call; for getting back up after failure; for soaring when others stayed grounded; for believing when you had every reason to quit. This book is my offering to your courage.

And, finally, to the One who makes flight possible—to my Savior, Pilot, Wind, Lift, Compass, and Safe Landing—Jesus Christ. Thank You for never leaving me in the valley, for calling me to the heights, and for reminding me every day that I was born to soar.

PREFACE

You were created to soar. Not just to take off—but to stay in the air, to overcome turbulence, and to reach your God-ordained destination in full flight.

In this powerful and prophetic work, Pastor Claudine Benjamin takes readers on an inspiring journey into the realm of spiritual altitude—where vision is clear, distractions fall away, and destiny becomes undeniable. Drawing deep parallels between natural flight and spiritual growth, In Full Flight will challenge and stretch you, and awaken the eagle within.

Through the symbolic lives of three uniquely crafted characters—Eli, the Young Eagle; Zara, the Soaring Eagle; and Obed, the Weathered Eagle—you will find your own experience mirrored. Each represents a different season of life and faith: the stage of learning to trust your wings, the height of purposeful soaring, and the tests of endurance through storms and aging skies.

This book is for:

- The believer who's just learning how to navigate the skies of faith.

- The visionary who's flying high but needs clarity and strategy to maintain momentum.

- The weary warrior who's been through spiritual storms and needs healing, rest, and perspective.

- The grounded soul who once soared but feels stuck, aimless, or afraid to fly again.

With each chapter, you will explore critical truths about spiritual and personal development, including:

- How to reach and maintain spiritual altitude without burning out.

- How to cope with disturbances in flight, from emotional turbulence and spiritual warfare to unexpected life shifts.

- How to break free from limiting beliefs, distractions, and generational ceilings that keep you grounded.

- How to recognize the difference between a temporary delay and a divine redirection.

- How to discern the voice of God—your Divine Pilot—in seasons of silence, storms, or sudden shifts.

- How to navigate transitions, transformation, and triumph in every stage of your journey.

You will gain theological depth and practical guidance—spiritual flight lessons that equip you to rise above adversity, navigate spiritual winds, and embrace your calling without fear. Through powerful scripture, prophetic insight, real-life wisdom, and reflective prompts, Pastor Claudine Benjamin gives you a front-row seat to your own spiritual evolution.

By the end of this book, you won't just believe you can fly—you will know how to stay in flight, how to stabilize when life shakes, how to rise above limitations, and how to finish your flight with purpose and power.

This is not just a book—it is your boarding pass to divine destiny. It is your flight manual for purpose. It is time to break the spiritual speed limits, defeat gravity, and ascend. You were born to soar—In Full Flight.

TABLE OF CONTENTS

About the Author iii

Dedication and Acknowledgments v

Preface vii

Introduction 13

Chapter 1: Understanding The Flight Plan 17

Chapter 2: Divine Design And Purpose 27

Chapter 3: Grounded But Not Defeated 39

Chapter 4: Achieving Altitude – The Takeoff Phase 45

Chapter 5: Climbing Above The Clouds 51

Chapter 6: Soaring At New Levels 57

Chapter 7: The Role Of The Holy Spirit In Your Flight ... 63

Chapter 8: Spiritual Navigation And Maintenance 71

Chapter 9: I'm Anointed To Soar Like An Eagle 79

Chapter 10: The Eagles Among Us 87

Chapter 11: The Eagle And The Storm 99

Chapter 12: When The Eagle Loses Its Feathers 103

Chapter 13: When You Are in Full Flight—Naturally And Spiritually
.... 109

Chapter 14: What Causes The Plane To Fly High   - With Spiritual
Insights 117

Chapter 15: What Do We Need Spiritually To Fly? 125

Chapter 16: Disturbances In Flight And How To Handle Them Successfully 131

Chapter 17: Coping With Disturbances In Full Flight – Spiritually And Physically 145

Chapter 18: The Dangers Of Mid-Flight Drift 157

Chapter 19: Midair Maintenance 163

Chapter 20: Knowing When To Descend 167

Chapter 21: Purpose Unfolded in Motion 175

Chapter 22: Inspiring Others to Take the Flight 183

Chapter 23: Leaving Flight Paths For Future Generations 189

Chapter 24: Landing In Purpose 195

Chapter 25: Identifying Your Eagle Type 201

Conclusion 205

The Sky Is Still Calling 205

INTRODUCTION

There is something breathtaking about the image of an eagle in flight—wings stretched wide, eyes fixed on the horizon, and strength undeterred by the winds beneath it. The eagle does not flap in panic; it soars with confidence. It rises higher, not by fleeing the storm, but by harnessing the very winds that threaten its peace.

This book, In Full Flight, is about that kind of rise—a rise into purpose, divine assignment, spiritual maturity, and ultimately, into the life God has destined for you. It is not just about taking off—it's about maintaining altitude. It's about not crashing mid-flight, not settling below the clouds, and not quitting because of turbulence. It's about what it takes to stay elevated in every area of your life.

As you read, you will journey alongside three symbolic eagles—Eli, the Young Eagle just discovering the power of his wings; Zara, the Soaring Eagle, flying strong and determined in her purpose; and Obed, the Weathered Eagle, seasoned by storms, scarred by experience, but wiser and higher because of it. Each one represents a phase in your journey—whether you are learning to leave the nest, rising into new heights, or flying through weariness and warfare. Their stories are your stories.

We live in a world full of noise, pressure, and spiritual gravity constantly trying to pull us down. But you were created to defy that

Pastor Dr. Claudine Benjamin

pull. You were born to soar, not settle. You were designed by God to fly above fear, anxiety, failure, trauma, stagnation, and sin. You are not earthbound. You have been given wings of faith, hope, purpose, and power.

This book draws inspiration from Isaiah 40:31, which promises that *"they that wait upon the Lord shall renew their strength; they shall mount up with wings as eagles..."* That verse is not a poetic metaphor—it is a divine blueprint for a life of forward motion, focused vision, and heavenly acceleration.

Throughout these pages, we will explore:

- What it means to reach spiritual altitude and why many never do.

- How to navigate disturbances like spiritual warfare, emotional burnout, and life transitions.

- How to maintain focus and balance when visibility is low and the pressure is high.

- What to do when you feel stuck in mid-air, unsure whether to climb higher or land.

- How to discern when it's time to rest, renew, or soar again.

We will study the natural principles of flight and the supernatural truths of scripture that empower us to live with divine momentum. You will learn how to align with the Holy Spirit—your eternal

In Full Flight

wind—and how to hear the voice of your Pilot, even when the cabin shakes.

This book is also for the tired soul who wonders, *"Why do I keep crashing?"* or the person who feels like they've been circling the same mountain, never arriving at purpose. If that's you, take heart. The problem is not your wings—it may be your weight, wind, or willingness to trust the Pilot. But the flight is not over.

So, buckle in. Prepare for elevation. Expect disruption. Welcome transformation. This journey will challenge, stretch, and awaken you. It's time to break spiritual ceilings, overcome emotional turbulence, and step fully into the altitude God has called you to.

Welcome to the flight of your life—In Full Flight.

— Pastor Claudine Benjamin

CHAPTER 1

UNDERSTANDING THE FLIGHT PLAN

TRUSTING GOD'S TIMING, DIRECTION, AND PROCESS

Every eagle in flight follows an invisible yet intentional path—a flight plan guided by instinct, pressure, and natural rhythm. In the same way, every believer has a spiritual flight plan—a divinely authored journey that includes your direction, timing, and process. Understanding that plan is critical to maintaining altitude, avoiding unnecessary detours, and completing your God-ordained mission.

You were not sent into the sky to wing it. You were sent to walk in step with divine coordinates. Your calling is not random—it's strategic. But for you to soar with clarity and confidence, you must trust the One who created you.

THE PILOT AND THE PLANNER

God is not only your Provider—He's your Pilot and Planner. He wrote your story before you took your first breath. Your purpose didn't begin when you figured out what you were good at. It began

17

Pastor Dr. Claudine Benjamin

when God formed you in the womb and whispered destiny over your life.

Jeremiah 29:11 reminds us: *"For I know the thoughts that I think toward you, saith the Lord..."*

Proverbs 16:9 says: *"A man's heart deviseth his way: but the Lord directeth his steps."*

You may not always understand the path, but you can trust the One who paved it. God's plan for your life includes where you take off, how you ascend, what you fly over, and when you land.

FLIGHT REQUIRES SUBMISSION TO PROCESS

Every pilot knows that flight isn't just about destination—it's about process.

Before you fly, you must:

1. Fuel up – Spiritually, this is prayer, fasting, and time in the Word.

2. Run your checks – Examine your heart, motives, and alignment.

3. Listen to the tower – You need divine clearance before taking off.

4. Know your route – You need a vision from God, not just personal ambition.

In Full Flight

Many try to skip this and fly on impulse or emotion. But an eagle that launches without preparation can burn out or fall. God's process may seem slow, but it's strategic.

Isaiah 28:10 says, *"...precept upon precept; line upon line..."* That's how He builds. Step by step. Level by level. Wind by wind.

Flight Insight: The right path at the wrong time becomes the wrong flight.

COURSE CORRECTIONS ARE PART OF THE JOURNEY

Even with a plan, flight requires constant adjustment. Winds shift. Clouds move. Visibility changes. And so must the pilot.

God will often allow course corrections in your life for:

- Sudden redirections
- Closed doors
- Delays that make no sense

DISRUPTIONS THAT FEEL LIKE FAILURE

But here's the truth: God is not punishing you—He's positioning you. What feels like a detour is often divine realignment. What seems like a delay is often God's way of keeping you from spiritual turbulence.

Pastor Dr. Claudine Benjamin

You don't need to panic—you need to trust the Tower. The Holy Spirit sees what you can't see. He knows what's in the airspace ahead.

Flight Insight: Adjustments are not always signs you're off course—they're signs He loves you enough to guide you.

FOLLOW THE SPIRITUAL ALTIMETER

An eagle knows how high it can fly based on internal signals. In the same way, God gives you spiritual altimeters—indicators that help you track your altitude, discern your atmosphere, and know when it's time to rise or rest.

These include:

- Peace – Is this flight birthed in anxiety or alignment?
- Conviction – Is God tugging you to wait, shift, or let go?
- Confirmation – Are there signs in His Word, in wise counsel, and through prayer that affirm this direction?

Too many believers fly blind. They ignore the Spirit's nudges and end up in storms they could have avoided. But those who listen to the internal gauges of the Spirit fly longer, stronger, and safer.

Flight Insight: Peace is not the absence of challenge—it's the presence of alignment.

OBEDIENCE IS YOUR NAVIGATION SYSTEM

The best navigation system in the kingdom is obedience. You don't have to know every detail—you just need to say yes to the next step.

Abraham didn't know the full map—he just left when God said go.

Noah didn't know how long the flood would last—he just obeyed the building instructions.

Mary didn't understand the full weight of her calling—she simply said, *"Be it unto me according to Your word."*

Your flight plan unfolds as you obey. It's not fully revealed at takeoff—it's given step by step, mile by mile, cloud by cloud.

Flight Insight: Don't wait for full clarity to take your first step. Obey the last thing God told you.

SOAR ACCORDING TO THE SCRIPT

Your life was not meant to be reactionary—it was meant to be revelatory. You are not flying aimlessly. You are following a divine script authored by the One who sees the end from the beginning.

Yes, the skies may be unpredictable. But the flight plan is still firm.

Trust it.
Lean into it.
Let the Holy Spirit be your compass and your current.

Because when you fly according to the plan, you won't just reach your destination—you will transform others along the way.

Pastor Dr. Claudine Benjamin

THE ANATOMY OF A SOARING LIFE

DISCOVERING YOUR NATURAL AND SPIRITUAL WINGS – CREATED TO FLY, NOT CRAWL

Before a bird ever takes flight, it is already equipped with the tools to soar. The design is intentional. The wings are not random. The frame, feathers, hollow bones, and instinct all point to one undeniable truth: this creature was created to fly. Likewise, the anatomy of your life—your personality, gifts, pain, process, and calling—were all divinely designed to take you higher.

You were not born to crawl through life, dragging the weight of the past or living beneath the potential planted within you. You were created to rise, move in purpose, and fulfill destiny. The problem is, too many people settle for walking when they were built to soar.

DISCOVERING YOUR WINGS: THE UNSEEN

POTENTIAL

A young eagle doesn't fly immediately after hatching. At first, it's awkward, unsure, and grounded. But within its genetic makeup is the full potential to rule the skies. The same is true for you. God placed greatness in your design long before you realized it.

Sometimes life has a way of clipping our wings before we even realize we have them. Childhood trauma, rejection, insecurity, failure, and fear can all cause us to doubt our ability to rise. But discovering your wings is about awakening what God already placed inside of you.

In Full Flight

You may not feel strong, but you're equipped. You may not look ready, but you're already anointed. You were created to fly—not just spiritually but purposefully, emotionally, and mentally.

Flight Reminder: If you have wings, crawling is not your destiny.

NATURAL WINGS: YOUR PERSONALITY, GIFTS, AND PASSIONS

Your natural "wings" are the tools God gave you at birth—your talents, intellect, passion, creativity, leadership, and unique voice. These aren't accidental; they are evidence of divine intention. What you're naturally good at isn't random—it's often the clue to what you're called to. But just like wings must be stretched and strengthened before flight, your gifts must be developed and disciplined. Natural ability without spiritual direction is dangerous. It can lead to pride or perversion of purpose.

Flight Insight: Don't hide your wings because others are afraid to fly.

SPIRITUAL WINGS: ANOINTED TO SOAR

While natural wings help you move forward, spiritual wings help you rise above. These wings are developed through relationship with God—through the Word, worship, prayer, fasting, and obedience. They are the tools that allow you to soar above anxiety, sin, distraction, and doubt.

Pastor Dr. Claudine Benjamin

The Holy Spirit is the wind beneath your spiritual wings. Without Him, you may flap, but you will never truly soar. He gives you clarity, power, perspective, and supernatural endurance.

Zara, the soaring eagle, reminds young Eli: *"Wings alone don't take you higher—it's the wind you trust to carry you."* Likewise, trusting in your own strength will only take you so far. Trust in God will take you beyond what you can imagine.

Flight Insight: With spiritual wings, storms don't stop you—they lift you.

CREATED TO FLY, NOT CRAWL

Some people spend their lives adapting to low places they were never meant to live in. They crawl through relationships, careers, and seasons that suppress their design. But the truth is clear: you were made to fly.

Eagles don't chase chickens. They don't explain their wings to creatures who were never called to soar. They don't apologize for their altitude. Neither should you.

You weren't created to stay grounded in fear. You weren't created to walk in circles of confusion. You weren't created to survive— you were created to soar.

EMBRACE YOUR WINGS; EMBRACE YOUR WHY

The anatomy of a soaring life is rooted in awareness—knowing what God placed inside you, how to develop it, and when to use it.

24

In Full Flight

Your wings are already there. Now it's time to stretch them, trust the wind of God, and rise into your calling.

Crawling is beneath your design. You were created to fly. So spread your wings, beloved—you haven't even reached your highest altitude yet.

ELI THE YOUNG EAGLE – THE SEEKER OF THE SKIES

Symbolism: Discovery of identity and early spiritual awakening.

Profile: Eli is a curious young eagle who knows he's made for more than the nest. Though others are content to stay grounded, Eli senses the wind calling him higher. He represents the reader's early awareness of divine purpose and the tension between comfort and calling.

ZARA THE SOARING EAGLE – THE ALTITUDE KEEPER

Symbolism: Consistency, focus, and spiritual discipline.

Profile: Zara has mastered the art of flight. She knows how to ride the wind and avoid unnecessary battles. She represents the believer who has matured and learned to maintain altitude through spiritual practices and discernment.

OBED THE WEATHERED EAGLE – THE WISE GUIDE

Symbolism: Resilience, legacy, and renewal.

Pastor Dr. Claudine Benjamin

Profile: Obed has survived many storms, but instead of retiring in defeat, he chooses to renew his strength. He undergoes the painful process of transformation—plucking out old feathers and sharpening his beak—to continue soaring. Obed represents legacy, the power of renewal, and the wisdom that comes through endurance.

PRAYER

Heavenly Father, I thank You for designing a flight plan unique to my destiny. Help me to seek Your guidance daily, trusting that every detail of my journey is under Your divine control. When I feel uncertain, remind me that You are the Author and Finisher of my faith. Teach me to align my steps with Your Word and to rest in the assurance that You are always directing my path. I yield my plans to Your will and submit to Your greater purpose.

Scripture: Proverbs 3:5-6 – "Trust in the Lord with all thine heart; and lean not unto thine own understanding. In all thy ways acknowledge him, and he shall direct thy paths."

CHAPTER 2

DIVINE DESIGN AND PURPOSE

YOU WERE MADE FOR THE HEIGHTS – ALIGNING YOUR VISION WITH GOD'S PLAN

You are not a mistake. You are not random. You were crafted—carefully, intentionally, and divinely—by the hand of the Creator Himself. Every detail of your being, from your natural instincts to your deepest passions, was built with purpose. You were made to soar.

Just as the eagle is uniquely designed for high-altitude flight, so are you uniquely formed for kingdom elevation. Eagles don't fly like sparrows. They don't dwell in low places. Their entire makeup—from their hollow bones to their expansive wingspan—is a testimony of design meeting destiny.

You were made for the heights. But to rise, you must understand not only who you are but *whose* you are.

THE MARK OF DIVINE INTENTIONALITY

Everything about you points to divine design:

- Your gifts were given on purpose.

Pastor Dr. Claudine Benjamin

- Your story was allowed with purpose.
- Your calling exists for a greater purpose.

Nothing in your life is wasted—not even the pain. The moments you thought disqualified you were actually shaping you for your flight. God is a master builder, and nothing He designs is without meaning.

Psalm 139:16 (NLT) says, *"You saw me before I was born. Every day of my life was recorded in your book..."*

You weren't designed for survival—you were designed for assignment. Purpose is not a side effect of salvation—it's a foundational part of it.

Flight Insight: The enemy doesn't attack what's random. He attacks what's *intended*.

YOU WERE MADE FOR THE HEIGHTS

You don't need to manufacture significance—you need to *discover* it. The eagle doesn't try to be what it's not. It doesn't envy the peacock's beauty or the owl's mystery. It soars in its own authority. That's your invitation: to own the high places God made for *you*.

High places aren't always glamorous. They come with:

- Isolation for revelation.
- Higher winds that require stronger wings.
- A broader view that demands greater responsibility.

But they also come with:

28

- Divine perspective.
- Supernatural strength.
- Deeper intimacy with God.

It's in the high places that Moses received the commandments. It's where Jesus was transfigured. It's where vision gets clarified and distractions fall away.

Flight Insight: Elevation reveals both your calling and your character.

ALIGNING YOUR VISION WITH GOD'S PLAN

Vision is the compass of your calling. Without it, you wander. With it, you soar.

Eagles have extraordinary vision. They can see prey from miles away. Spiritually, vision is not just about what you *see* but how you *perceive* what you see. Your vision must be shaped by the Word, directed by the Holy Spirit, and surrendered to God's timing.

Proverbs 29:18 says, *"Where there is no vision, the people perish…"*

The world offers ambition. God gives *vision*. They are not the same.

Ambition says, "Climb at any cost."
Vision says, "Fly when the wind of God says go."

Ambition exhausts you. Vision sustains you.

Pastor Dr. Claudine Benjamin

To align your vision with God's plan:

- Spend time in His Word.
- Stay accountable to spiritual mentors.
- Seek confirmation in prayer and peace.
- Trust God's no just as much as His yes.

Flight Insight: Vision without God becomes a distraction. Vision with God becomes destiny.

DON'T SETTLE IN THE NEST

Many never soar because they become too comfortable in the nest. It's safe. It's familiar. But it's not permanent.

The nest was only meant to *develop* you, not *define* you.

There comes a moment in every eagle's life when the nest is stirred—thorns are added, space is reduced, and comfort is removed. Why? Because the eagle is ready to fly, even if it doesn't feel like it.

God will stir your comfort to awaken your calling.

You may be in a season right now where everything feels like it's shifting, and you're unsure why. Could it be that you're being prepared for takeoff?

Flight Insight: When the nest becomes uncomfortable, it's a sign that elevation is near.

30

DESIGNED FOR DESTINY

You were born with wings—natural and spiritual—and it's time to use them. You don't have to force your flight. You simply have to align with the One who designed it.

God is not asking you to soar in your own strength. He's asking you to trust His design, submit to His direction, and rise into His destiny for your life.

You were *anointed* for the airspace you're called to.

So stretch your wings.
Lift your eyes.

YOU WERE MADE FOR THE HEIGHTS – ALIGNING YOUR VISION WITH GOD'S PLAN

*"Before I formed thee in the belly I knew thee; and before thou camest forth out of the womb I sanctified thee, and I ordained thee a prophet unto the nations." — **Jeremiah 1:5***

From the very beginning, you were **designed to fly.** Not in the natural sense, but in the spiritual realm—you were created for altitude. God didn't fashion you to live grounded by fear, bound by insecurity, or tethered by the opinions of others. You were handcrafted with **purpose**, shaped with **vision**, and infused with **divine potential**. He carved into your very being the ability to rise—**above obstacles, above mediocrity, and above limitations**.

Pastor Dr. Claudine Benjamin

DESIGNED TO SOAR: YOUR IDENTITY COMES FROM ABOVE

Before you were born—before you ever took your first breath—God had already spoken **purpose over your life.** Your design is not random; it is intentional. Just like the eagle is designed to soar high with its wide wingspan, powerful vision, and resilient feathers, so too were you designed with everything you need to reach your God-given altitude.

Your divine design includes:

- **Spiritual wings** to lift you into realms of faith, revelation, and boldness.

- **Vision** to see beyond the natural—to perceive what others cannot.

- **Inner strength** to withstand pressure, resistance, and elevation without collapsing.

- **Spiritual instincts** to know when to rise, when to rest, and when to wait for the wind of God.

God doesn't create anything without a purpose. You are not a mistake. You are not "extra." You were *engineered* by heaven to accomplish things only **you** can fulfill. The first step to flying high is **believing in the brilliance of your design**.

32

YOU WERE MADE FOR THE HEIGHTS

"For thou hast made him a little lower than the angels, and hast crowned him with glory and honour. Thou madest him to have dominion over the works of thy hands; thou hast put all things under his feet:" —**Psalm 8:5–6**

Some believers settle for spiritual survival when they are called to spiritual dominion. Many live in the valley of comparison, doubt, or fear—never realizing they were created to **dwell in the high places**.

But here's a truth you must grasp deeply: **Elevation is your inheritance.** The mountaintop life is not reserved for the elite few—it's for every child of God who chooses to align with His plan, rise in faith, and trust the process.

Characteristics of those called to spiritual heights:

- They think differently (see Romans 12:2).
- They pray boldly (see James 5:16).
- They act in obedience (see Isaiah 1:19).
- They embrace discipline (see Hebrews 12:11).
- They do not fear the winds (see Isaiah 40:31).

Eagles don't fly with pigeons. When you were made for the heights, you can't find peace in low places. **You'll feel restless, out of place, and even agitated** when you're surrounded by small vision or low expectations.

Pastor Dr. Claudine Benjamin

Your spirit knows what you were built for—even if your mind hasn't caught up yet.

VISION VERSUS SIGHT: SEEING THROUGH GOD'S EYES

Sight is what you see with your natural eyes. Vision is what God allows you to see through faith.

"Where there is no vision, the people perish..." — **Proverbs 29:18**

Vision is essential for divine flight. Pilots rely on instruments and clear direction when flying through clouds. In the same way, you must develop spiritual clarity—the ability to hear and obey God's direction when nothing around you looks certain.

Aligning with God's vision includes:

- Praying for discernment, not just direction.
- Surrendering your preferences for God's priorities.
- Letting go of small goals to embrace a kingdom mindset.
- Trusting the process even when the pathway is hidden.

God's plan may not always match your original expectations—but it will always exceed your imagination. **When your vision aligns with His, momentum is inevitable.**

THE DANGER OF MISALIGNMENT

Many believers crash, not because they don't have wings but because they fly on their own terms.

Misalignment looks like:

- Pursuing purpose outside of God's timing.
- Comparing your journey to someone else's.
- Carrying people or burdens that God never assigned.
- Letting fear dictate your altitude.
- Trusting your ambition over the Holy Spirit's guidance.

Just as a plane out of alignment risks falling from the sky, so too do we when we step out of God's will. **Alignment is the difference between motion and momentum** between activity and anointing.

You weren't created to fly in circles or crash repeatedly. You were called to **rise, glide, and land in destiny**.

HOW TO ALIGN WITH GOD'S PLAN

Here's how you recalibrate when you feel off-course:

1. Surrender Fully

Lay your will at the altar. The greatest altitude you'll ever achieve begins with humility.

"not my will, but thine, be done." —**Luke 22:42**

2. Seek God Daily

Make His voice the loudest in your life. Seek Him in prayer, in the Word, and through spiritual mentors.

Pastor Dr. Claudine Benjamin

"In all thy ways acknowledge him, and he shall direct thy paths."
—**Proverbs 3:6**

3. Obey Without Delay

Partial or delayed obedience is still disobedience. Move when He says move. Wait when He says wait.

" If ye be willing and obedient, ye shall eat the good of the land:"
—**Isaiah 1:19**

4. Trust the Pilot

Even when the journey doesn't make sense. Even when the turbulence is heavy. Even when the sky is dark.

"The steps of a good man are ordered by the Lord."
>   —**A Life of Purpose is a Life of Flight**

You weren't created for wandering. You were created for **intentional flight**. Every gift, trial, and lesson has been shaping you to fly **in alignment with heaven's purpose**.

When you understand your divine design, embrace your altitude, and align with God's plan, **your life takes on supernatural momentum**. Things begin to click. Doors begin to open. Strength replaces striving. And even when storms come, your vision keeps you steady.

This is your season to fly **not just high—but aligned.**

36

PRAYER

Lord, I glorify You for the intentional design You placed upon my life. Before I was formed, You knew me. May I walk confidently in the purpose You've ordained, understanding that I am fearfully and wonderfully made. Let every doubt be silenced by the truth of who I am in You. Reveal more of my purpose each day, and help me to embrace it fully, knowing that my identity and assignment are rooted in You.

Scripture: *"Before I formed thee in the belly I knew thee; and before thou camest forth out of the womb I sanctified thee, and I ordained thee a prophet unto the nations."* —**Jeremiah 1:5**

CHAPTER 3

GROUNDED BUT NOT DEFEATED

WHEN LIFE KEEPS YOU ON THE RUNWAY – IDENTIFYING WEIGHTS THAT HOLD YOU DOWN

Before any plane takes off, it must pass through the runway—a long stretch of ground that feels more like waiting than flying. For many, this season of life is frustrating. You see others in the sky. You hear the call to soar. But you feel stuck—*grounded*. Delayed. Overlooked. Left behind.

Let this be your reminder: **Grounded does not mean defeated.**

You may be in a season where nothing seems to be moving. Your dreams feel stalled. Your purpose feels foggy. But God has not forgotten you. The runway is not a punishment—it's a place of *preparation*.

WHEN LIFE KEEPS YOU ON THE RUNWAY

Every eagle must learn to build strength before taking flight. Its wings must develop the power to sustain it, not just lift it. The waiting season—your runway—teaches you:

Pastor Dr. Claudine Benjamin

- Endurance
- Perspective
- Patience
- Discipline

You may feel like you've been sitting too long. You're flapping your wings in faith, but there is no lift yet. This season of delay could be:

- A divine holding pattern for your safety.
- A sacred moment to reinforce your foundation.
- A pruning process to remove distractions.
- A waiting zone while God opens the right airspace.

Even the strongest planes can't take off until **air traffic control clears the way.** So it is in the Spirit. God may be delaying your launch to keep you from crashing into someone else's unhealed debris.

Flight Insight: Don't despise the runway. It's where pilots are trained, and destinies are refined.

GROUNDED BUT STILL GROWING

Being grounded doesn't mean God has benched you. It means He's building you. Just because you aren't visible in the sky doesn't mean you aren't valuable to the kingdom. Your greatest growth often happens in hidden places.

Ask Joseph. Before he led Egypt, he was hidden in a pit and forgotten in prison.

40

In Full Flight

Ask Moses. Before he led Israel, he was tending sheep in obscurity for forty years.

Ask Jesus. Before He launched into public ministry, He waited thirty years in preparation.

If God is keeping you grounded, it's because your launch is too important to rush.

Flight Insight: God doesn't send unprepared eagles into heavy airspace.

IDENTIFYING WEIGHTS THAT HOLD YOU DOWN

Sometimes what's grounding you isn't God's timing—it's the *weights you refuse to release.*

Hebrews 12:1 says, *"Let us strip off every weight that slows us down, especially the sin that so easily trips us up..."* —**NLT**

You can't fly high while carrying low-level burdens. What you tolerate on the ground will sabotage you in the sky.

Common weights that hinder flight:

1. **Unforgiveness** – Bitterness is heavy and poisons your altitude.
2. **Fear** – Fear of failure, fear of success, fear of judgment. It grounds your boldness.
3. **Comparison** – Looking at other eagles distracts you from your own wings.

41

Pastor Dr. Claudine Benjamin

4. **Guilt and Shame** – When you believe you're disqualified, you stop trying to rise.
5. **Toxic Relationships** – Some people are not your passengers—they're anchors.

Ask yourself:

- What's weighing me down that God never asked me to carry?
- Who am I dragging along that doesn't want to fly?
- What thought pattern keeps me afraid to launch?

God's desire is not just that you fly—it's that you fly *free*.

Flight Insight: Your wings are ready. Your spirit is willing. But the weights must go.

THE POWER OF STAYING READY

The hardest part of being grounded is feeling forgotten. But God never wastes a waiting season.

While you're on the runway, stay:

- **In prayer** – This keeps your vision clear.
- **In preparation** – Keep learning, growing, and developing.
- **In praise** – This keeps your altitude in check before you ever leave the ground.

Eagles don't run when they're grounded—they rest and recalibrate.

So, if you're grounded today, don't quit. Don't shrink. Don't sulk. Let God do what He needs to do beneath the surface so when the call comes—you're ready.

DELAY IS NOT DEFEAT

Being grounded is hard. But it's not hopeless.

You are not forgotten.
You are not finished.
You are not too late.

There is still purpose in your wings. There is still fire in your flight. And when the time is right, the same God who called you to soar will open the runway and clear the skies.

Until then, stand strong.
Pray hard.
Release the weights.
Because when the moment comes, you'll rise higher than you've ever imagined.

PRAYER

Father, even in seasons when I feel grounded, I thank You that I am not defeated. Let my waiting be purposeful, and my grounding become preparation for the next ascent. Renew my hope, Lord, and strengthen my resolve to rise again. Like the eagle, I will mount up on wings with Your strength and soar above every circumstance that try to hold me back.

Pastor Dr. Claudine Benjamin

Scripture: Isaiah 40:31 – "But they that wait upon the Lord shall renew their strength; they shall mount up with wings as eagles; they shall run, and not be weary; and they shall walk, and not faint."

CHAPTER 4

ACHIEVING ALTITUDE – THE TAKEOFF PHASE

FAITH AS YOUR LIFT-OFF POWER – BREAKING THROUGH THE RESISTANCE

The moment between being grounded and taking off is one of the most critical—and most misunderstood—phases in the flight of purpose. It's the moment when momentum must meet movement, when belief must be activated, and when faith becomes your engine. This is *the takeoff phase*—when everything you've been preparing for is tested in motion.

Many people get stuck at this stage. They're equipped. They're called. They even believe. But they never leave the ground because they hesitate at the edge of obedience. Fear grips them. Doubt clouds them. Resistance pressures them.

But if you want to soar, you must *take off*.

You cannot reach spiritual altitude without movement. And you can't rely on your strength alone. You need *faith*—the supernatural lift God gives when you trust Him to launch you into the unknown.

45

Pastor Dr. Claudine Benjamin

FAITH IS YOUR LIFT-OFF POWER

In aviation, lift-off is the result of two things: **thrust and lift**. Without thrust, the plane sits still. Without lift, it stays on the ground. Spiritually, **faith is your thrust** and **obedience is your lift**. **Hebrews 11:1** says, *"Now faith is the substance of things hoped for, the evidence of things not seen."*

Faith is not just believing God exists—it's trusting Him enough to move when you don't see how it will work. It's flapping your wings in a sky you have never flown before. It's stepping out before the road appears.

Flight Insight: Faith without movement is admiration—not activation.

Faith says:

- "I may not see the full sky, but I trust the One who made it."
- "I don't have all the details, but I'll move with what God gave me."
- "The wind may be unpredictable, but my calling is undeniable."

When God calls you to take off, He's not looking for perfection— He's looking for *participation*.

THE TAKEOFF PHASE: A DEFINING MOMENT

The takeoff phase requires courage. This is the moment when everything shifts:

In Full Flight

- From dreaming to doing.
- From preparing to producing.
- From fear to flight.

Every eagle must eventually leap. Even with wobbly wings. Even with a racing heart. There comes a moment when you must launch.

It is in the takeoff that you prove to yourself—and to every enemy that tried to ground you—that your wings *work*.

What defines this phase?

- **Decision** – Will I obey or delay?
- **Determination** – Will I push through or pull back?
- **Dependence** – Will I rely on God or return to comfort?

Many fail to soar, not because they are not called—but because they never *left the ground.*

Flight Insight: Takeoff doesn't wait for comfort—it responds to calling.

BREAKING THROUGH THE RESISTANCE

Every takeoff meets **resistance**. In fact, planes **must push against the wind** to lift off. So must you.

Resistance may come in the form of:

- Fear of failure.
- Criticism from others.

47

Pastor Dr. Claudine Benjamin

- Financial limitations.
- Insecurity or inadequacy.
- Inner voices telling you "you're not ready."

But here's the paradox: resistance is not your enemy—it's your launching force.

Eagles use the resistance of the wind to rise. Without wind, they glide. With wind, they ascend. What pushes against you can actually lift you if you use it right.

- That rejection? It pushed you into purpose.
- That closed door? It redirected you to the right path.
- That disappointment? It trained your wings for strength.

James 1:2–4 reminds us that trials produce endurance. And endurance matures your flight.

Flight Insight: If the wind is strong, don't panic—prepare to rise.

You can't avoid friction at takeoff—it's built into the design of flight. But with faith, you push through.

Consider:

- **Peter** had to step onto the water before he could walk in the miraculous.
- **Esther** had to risk death before she could save a nation.
- **Gideon** had to face his fears before he became a deliverer.

So do you.

48

Your first launch may feel awkward. You might question your ability. You might flap more than you glide. But keep going. Once you break through resistance, the atmosphere shifts. You gain altitude. You rise above the noise. And the wind that opposed you becomes the wind that *carries* you.

YOU WERE BUILT FOR TAKEOFF

The nest is not your destiny. The runway is not your prison. It's your launching pad.

Everything you have been through, every lesson you have learned, every moment of growth has led to this point: *the moment you decide to take off.*

God is not asking for perfection—He's asking for movement. So spread your wings. Engage your faith. Embrace the resistance. And *take flight.*

Because the sky is waiting.

And you, child of God, were never made to stay grounded.

You were *anointed to ascend.*

PRAYER

Lord God, as I step into my takeoff phase, I trust You to lift me above the past and into new spiritual heights. Give me the boldness to move forward, leaving behind fear and insecurity. Propel me by Your Spirit and fuel my ascent with unwavering faith. I declare that

Pastor Dr. Claudine Benjamin

I am ready for takeoff—fully aligned with Your wind beneath my wings.

Scripture: Psalm 18:33 – "He maketh my feet like hinds' feet, and setteth me upon my high places."

CHAPTER 5

CLIMBING ABOVE THE CLOUDS

TRUSTING GOD IN TURBULENCE – NAVIGATING UNSEEN REALMS

There comes a time in every eagle's flight when the skies grow thick and visibility fades. The sun is hidden, the wind becomes unpredictable, and the path ahead seems unclear. This is the moment when instinct alone is not enough—trust must take over.

Every believer will face this kind of moment—a moment where the presence of God seems veiled, your prayers feel unanswered, and the way forward is wrapped in spiritual fog. This is what we call turbulence—not the kind that shakes planes, but the kind that shakes your soul.

But just as the eagle climbs above the clouds to find stillness and clarity, you are also called to rise higher—not by sight, but by faith.

WHEN THE CLOUDS OBSTRUCT THE LIGHT

Clouds block what is above but don't remove its existence. The sun is still shining—you just can't see it. Spiritually, there will be

Pastor Dr. Claudine Benjamin

seasons where the clarity of God's voice feels dim, His direction feels delayed, and His presence feels distant.

You will wonder:

- "Did I miss God?"
- "Why is this so hard?"
- "What do I do when I can't see what's next?"

But this is the testing ground of trust. This is where spiritual maturity is developed—not when you're coasting through clear skies, but when you're flying blind and still choosing to trust.

2 Corinthians 5:7 says, *"For we walk by faith, not by sight."*

Flight Insight: Your faith is proven in the clouds—not beneath them.

TRUSTING GOD IN THE TURBULENCE

Turbulence is not always a sign something's wrong—it's a sign that you're moving. In fact, turbulence is most intense when planes change altitudes. The same is true spiritually. Whenever God is calling you higher, expect some resistance.

But here's the key: the turbulence may shake you, but it won't stop you—if you trust the One guiding your flight.

When you're facing turbulence:

- Trust God's timing, even when you feel delayed.
- Trust God's presence, even when you feel alone.

- Trust God's purpose, even when it looks unclear.

Ask the eagle—it doesn't flap harder in turbulence. It spreads its wings wider and lets the wind carry it. That's what God wants from you: less striving, more surrender.

"Thou wilt keep him in perfect peace, whose mind is stayed on thee: because he trusteth in thee." —**Isaiah 26:3**

Flight Insight: You're not called to fight the turbulence—you're called to ride the wind of trust.

NAVIGATING THE UNSEEN REALMS

The higher you go, the more invisible your path becomes. But just because it's unseen doesn't mean it's unguided.

God often calls us to move in realms we can't fully understand:

- A ministry assignment we feel unqualified for.
- A decision that goes against logic but aligns with faith.
- A release from something familiar into something unfamiliar.
- A deeper calling to prayer, intercession, or warfare.

This is where discernment becomes your compass. The deeper you go in God, the less visible the landmarks become. You begin relying not on what you see but what you sense in your spirit. This is the realm of prophetic movement—the unseen realm.

It is:

Pastor Dr. Claudine Benjamin

- The place of mystery.
- The place of intimacy.
- The place of trust.
- The place where God's voice becomes your map

You don't navigate the unseen with natural eyes—you navigate it through sensitivity to the Holy Spirit.

"But God hath revealed them unto us by his Spirit: for the Spirit searcheth all things, yea, the deep things of God." **—1 Corinthians 2:10**

Flight Insight: In the unseen realm, peace becomes your pilot, and presence becomes your path.

ABOVE THE CLOUDS IS WHERE CLARITY RESIDES

The beautiful truth is this: there is clarity above the clouds. The turbulence may last for a while. The vision may seem blurry. But if you don't panic—if you stay in flight, stay in faith, and stay in the Spirit—you'll rise above the storm.

Above the clouds:

- The sun is still shining.
- The atmosphere is calmer.
- The view is breathtaking.

This is what happens when you spiritually mature; you learn to climb higher instead of crashing in confusion. You press into worship when you don't feel like it. You pray when you don't hear

54

In Full Flight

anything back. You give when it feels like nothing's changing. And somehow, He lifts you.

— You were built for the heights, not the panic.
— You were made to trust God—even in spiritual fog.
— You were designed to soar—even when there is turbulence.
— You were equipped to rise—even when the sky is heavy.

So don't descend out of fear. Don't turn back because of shaking. Don't quit when the path seems invisible.

Spread your wings. Stay in position. Trust the wind.
Above the clouds—that's where you'll find your clarity.

PRAYER

Gracious God, thank You for the strength to rise above the weight of life's clouds. When the darkness tries to surround me, lift my eyes to Your light. Teach me to trust You beyond what I see and to have faith that takes me higher into Your presence. Just like the eagle climbs above the storm, help me to rise above fear, discouragement, and confusion, knowing that You dwell in the high places and have called me upward.

Scripture: Colossians 3:2 – "Set your affection on things above, not on things on the earth."

CHAPTER 6

SOARING AT NEW LEVELS

LIVING ABOVE LIFE'S STORMS – MAINTAINING CONSISTENT ALTITUDE

There is a difference between flying and soaring. Flying takes effort. Soaring takes alignment. Flying requires flapping. Soaring requires surrender. And soaring at new levels requires something greater: **spiritual maturity** and **a deeper trust in God.**

As you grow in Christ, God calls you to ascend to higher places— new dimensions of faith, new realms of purpose, deeper intimacy, and greater impact. But with every new level comes new challenges: increased resistance, unseen pressure, and a greater need for sustained altitude.

Just like the eagle, you are called not just to rise—but to **live** above the storm. And you're called not just to reach a level—but to **maintain it.**

Pastor Dr. Claudine Benjamin

SOARING AT NEW LEVELS: THE ELEVATION OF MATURITY

When God promotes you spiritually, He doesn't just elevate your influence—He deepens your capacity. Soaring at new levels isn't about chasing platforms—it's about stewarding altitude.

As you rise, you must learn:

- How to breathe at higher altitudes.
- How to hear God clearly above the noise.
- How to protect your peace.
- How to walk in humility despite new access.

New levels require **new disciplines**. What worked in the last season may not be enough for this one. You can't soar at new levels with old habits.

Flight Insight: With elevation comes expectation. Higher places require greater self-awareness and deeper dependence on God.

Soaring at new levels means:

- Praying deeper, not just louder.
- Serving with consistency, not just charisma.
- Trusting God's voice even when you don't get answers.
- Letting go of people, places, or patterns that can't go higher with you.

*"I press toward the mark for the prize of the high calling of God in Christ Jesus." —**Philippians 3:14***

In Full Flight

LIVING ABOVE LIFE'S STORMS

One of the most powerful traits of the eagle is its ability to **fly above storms**. While most birds seek shelter, the eagle ascends through the pressure system and glides **above the chaos**.

Soaring above the storm doesn't mean denying its existence—it means learning to **live above its impact.**

Storms will come:

- Financial storms.
- Relational storms.
- Health storms.
- Internal storms of fear, anxiety, and self-doubt.

But you were not designed to live at the level of your problems. You were **anointed to live at the level of your promise**.

Isaiah 43:2a says, *"When thou passest through the waters, I will be with thee; and through the rivers, they shall not overflow thee:"*

That doesn't mean you won't feel the rain—it means the storm won't control your flight. When you've learned to soar, your worship isn't silenced by the weather. Your peace isn't dictated by people. Your purpose isn't disrupted by pressure.

Flight Insight: The enemy wants to ground you with storms. God teaches you to use the wind.

Storms are not your stopping place—they are **your lifting place**.

59

Pastor Dr. Claudine Benjamin

MAINTAINING CONSISTENT ALTITUDE

Reaching a new level is one thing. **Staying there** is another.

Altitude without consistency becomes dangerous. A soaring eagle knows when to rise, when to rest, and how to adjust to subtle changes in the atmosphere. If it flaps too much, it wastes energy. If it glides too long, it loses elevation.

In your spiritual walk, maintaining consistent altitude requires:

- **Spiritual routines** – Daily prayer, fasting, worship, and time in the Word.
- **Mental discipline** – Guarding your thoughts and taking every imagination captive.
- **Emotional maturity** – Not reacting to everything, but remaining anchored in truth.
- **Relational wisdom** – Surrounding yourself with people who challenge you to grow.

*"And let us not be weary in well doing: for in due season we shall reap, if we faint not." —**Galatians 6:9***

God is looking for steady eagles—those who don't flap wildly when winds shift but who have learned to ride the flow of grace, peace, and purpose consistently.

Flight Insight: Consistency is what keeps you soaring when motivation fades.

ELEVATION WITH ENDURANCE

Many can ascend quickly—but few can endure the flight.

The key to soaring at new levels isn't talent—it's **tenacity.** It's staying committed even when it's not glamorous. It's showing up to the assignment even when it feels unnoticed. It's flying when it's lonely. It's soaring when you're tired.

But when you stay in the sky, something powerful happens—you begin to live with perspective. You see the world differently. You respond differently. And your altitude becomes your advantage.

— You no longer panic when storms form—you discern what God is doing in them.
— You no longer seek attention—you seek alignment.
— You don't live for applause—you live for assignment.

That's what it means to soar at new levels.

STAY HIGH; STAY ANCHORED

God didn't bring you this high to abandon you. But He also didn't elevate you so you could coast.

You are called to:

- Soar with power.
- Live with wisdom.
- Rise above life's storms.

Pastor Dr. Claudine Benjamin

Remain consistent in your altitude. So don't go back down. Don't apologize for the level God has brought you to. Don't settle into survival mode when you were made to glide in strength.

— **The sky is still calling.**
— **Your wings are still strong.**
— **And the Spirit is still lifting.**

Keep soaring.

CLOSING PRAYER

Lord, as You bring me to new levels, help me to remain humble and anchored in You. Elevation without You is empty, but with You, I will soar with purpose and power. Strengthen my wings of faith and remove any weights that hinder my rise. Let each new level be a platform to glorify You more and lead others to Your truth.

Scripture: Deuteronomy 32:11 – *"As an eagle stirreth up her nest, fluttereth over her young, spreadeth abroad her wings, taketh them, beareth them on her wings:"*

CHAPTER 7

THE ROLE OF THE HOLY SPIRIT IN YOUR FLIGHT

LETTING THE CAPTAIN TAKE CONTROL

Every eagle relies on instinct, environment, and experience—but in the spiritual realm, instinct is not enough. To soar at supernatural altitudes and fulfill your divine purpose, you must be guided by the Holy Spirit, the very breath of God Himself.

The Holy Spirit is more than a comforting presence. He is more than a gentle whisper in prayer. He is the Activator, Navigator, and Sustainer of your flight. Without Him, your wings may move but you won't gain spiritual momentum. With Him, the sky becomes your assignment, and every turn, climb, and descent comes with purpose and power.

THE SPIRIT WHO ACTIVATES AND ALIGNS

Before you take flight, the Holy Spirit works internally to activate your calling. He brings to life what God has placed inside of you. Gifts that lay dormant begin to stir. Desires for more of God begin

Pastor Dr. Claudine Benjamin

to increase—your appetite shifts from mere survival to spiritual fulfillment.

— He awakens passion for purpose.
— He breaks cycles of fear and stagnation.
— He initiates your divine momentum.

Just like the ignition in an airplane starts the engine, the Holy Spirit ignites your spiritual thrust. But He doesn't stop there—He also aligns you. So many believers are flapping in the wrong direction— chasing ambition, applause, or approval. But when you walk in the Spirit, He aligns your wings with heaven's wind. You stop striving and start soaring.

*"For as many as are led by the Spirit of God, they are the sons of God." —**Romans 8:14***

Flight Insight: Without activation, you won't move. Without alignment, you'll move in the wrong direction.

GUIDE IN DARK CLOUDS

Life isn't always sunny. Skies get cloudy. Direction becomes unclear. The enemy uses confusion to stall your flight—but the Holy Spirit breaks through the fog. He leads with precision, not panic.

John 16:13 says, *"Howbeit when he, the Spirit of truth, is come, he will guide you into all truth:"*

In Full Flight

He guides—not just to information, but to revelation. Truth isn't just a fact—it's a path. And the Holy Spirit is your GPS. When your vision is blocked, He becomes your compass.

You don't have to figure it all out. You don't need a detailed map. You need sensitivity. You need to trust the internal navigation of His presence.

When you are aligned with the Holy Spirit:

- You stop guessing.
- You start discerning.
- You stop chasing doors.
- You start walking through divine openings.

Flight Insight: The Holy Spirit doesn't always give explanations—He gives direction. Follow anyway.

COUNSELOR IN MOMENTS OF DOUBT

The takeoff may be thrilling, but turbulence can test your trust. The Holy Spirit becomes your counselor when anxiety tries to ground you. He speaks when fear is loud. He calms when chaos surrounds.

Isaiah 11:2 describes Him as the Spirit of counsel and might, wisdom and understanding.

He is the one who says:

- "You're not crazy—just called."
- "You're not failing—just forming."

65

Pastor Dr. Claudine Benjamin

- "You're not late—just being prepared."

When others don't understand your altitude, the Holy Spirit affirms your elevation. His voice is not always dramatic—but it is always divine.

Flight Insight: Let the Counselor counsel you before you consult the crowd.

FUEL WHEN YOU'RE TIRED

Even the strongest eagles get tired. Even the most anointed leaders feel drained. The flight can wear you out but the Holy Spirit is your fuel source.

— He renews your spiritual stamina.
— He breathes fresh wind when you're weary.
— He lifts your wings when you feel like quitting.

"The Spirit of God, who raised Jesus from the dead, lives in you. And just as God raised Christ Jesus from the dead, he will give life to your mortal bodies by this same Spirit living within you." — ***Romans 8:11 - NLT***

The same Spirit that raised Jesus doesn't just resurrect the dead—He restores the drained. You don't soar by willpower. You soar by wind power—the fresh wind of the Spirit moving through you.

Flight Insight: You can't fly long distances on yesterday's fuel. Stay filled.

CLARITY WHEN THE PATH IS FOGGY

The Holy Spirit brings not only direction but clarity. He makes the path clear when your circumstances are complicated. He silences fear's voice and amplifies truth.

When you don't know:

- Which door to take.
- When to move.
- Who to trust.
- Where to go next.

The Holy Spirit steps in and confirms what confusion tried to cloud.

Sometimes He speaks through peace. Sometimes through conviction. Sometimes through others. But His clarity never leads to chaos—it always leads to confidence.

"I will instruct you and teach you in the way you should go; I will counsel you with My eye upon you." —Psalm 32:8 - ESV

LET THE SPIRIT TAKE THE LEAD

You were never called to be your own pilot. The Holy Spirit is not your backup plan. He's not the last resort when plans fall apart. He's the Captain of your calling; the Wind beneath your wings, the Whisper behind your direction. So let Him lead. Let Him speak. Let Him strengthen. Let Him navigate. And watch how far, how high, and how purposefully you soar.

Pastor Dr. Claudine Benjamin

WIND BENEATH YOUR WINGS – HEARING HEAVEN'S GUIDANCE

Soaring isn't just about strength—it's about surrender. It's not just about effort—it's about alignment with the wind. And in the life of the believer, that wind is the **Holy Spirit.**

The Holy Spirit is not an accessory to the Christian walk—He is the essential force behind your flight. Without His presence, you will flap in frustration instead of gliding in grace. Without His voice, you will wander in circles instead of moving in precision. He is your **Divine Navigator**, your **Sustainer**, and your **Whisper of direction.**

You were never meant to soar alone. Your wings may carry you, but it's the **Spirit who lifts you.**

THE WIND BENEATH YOUR WINGS

Every eagle knows this: it doesn't fly by force—it soars by flow. It waits for wind patterns. It doesn't waste energy. It *waits* for lift. The Holy Spirit is the **invisible wind** beneath your wings.

He is:

- The one who lifts you when you feel like giving up.
- The one who pushes you higher when you're tired of trying.
- The one who whispers "You were made for more" when others say "settle."

68

Zechariah 4:6 reminds us: *"Not by might, nor by power, but by My Spirit, says the Lord of hosts." - ESV*

You don't soar by striving. You soar by surrender. You don't need more hustle—you need more Holy Spirit. When He lifts you, it's effortless. What once took flapping and straining, now happens through **divine alignment.**

How do you catch the wind?

- Daily communion through prayer.
- Creating space to listen, not just speak.
- Worship that shifts the atmosphere.
- Meditating on Scripture so your spirit becomes sensitized.

Flight Insight: When you ride the wind of the Spirit, you go farther with less strain.

PRAYER

Holy Spirit, be the wind beneath my wings. I surrender to Your direction and wisdom. Fill me with Your presence and teach me how to fly in alignment with the Father's will. When turbulence arises, may Your voice be louder than every distraction. Thank You for being my ever-present guide, comforter, and strength.

Scripture: John 14:26 – *"But the Comforter, which is the Holy Ghost, whom the Father will send in my name, he shall teach you all things, and bring all things to your remembrance, whatsoever I have said unto you."*

CHAPTER 8

SPIRITUAL NAVIGATION AND MAINTENANCE

HEARING HEAVEN'S GUIDANCE

Spiritual navigation requires **spiritual sensitivity**. You can't soar at high altitudes while tuned in to low-level noise. The Holy Spirit is speaking—but are you listening?

Romans 8:14 says, *"For as many as are led by the Spirit of God, they are the sons of God."*

To follow the Spirit, you must:

- Learn to **quiet the chaos** in your mind.
- Distinguish between emotion and revelation.
- Value stillness as much as activity.

The Holy Spirit doesn't scream—He **nudges**. He whispers in the quiet moments, convicts gently when you're off course, and confirms truth through peace. If your world is always noisy, you'll miss the signals.

71

Pastor Dr. Claudine Benjamin

Signs you're hearing heaven:

- You experience peace that makes no sense.
- Scripture aligns with what you're sensing.
- You're drawn into deeper levels of obedience.
- Godly counsel echoes what you're hearing in prayer.

If you're unsure what you're hearing—*pause*. The Holy Spirit never pressures. He guides. He corrects. He comforts. And He leads with wisdom that won't leave you confused.

Flight Insight: Hearing God is not about volume—it's about intimacy.

MAINTAINING YOUR SPIRITUAL ALTITUDE

Once you've soared with the Spirit, you must maintain that altitude. The higher you go, the more intentional you must be about spiritual maintenance.

This includes:

- **Consistent prayer** (your spiritual communication system).
- **Fasting** (removing static that blocks the signal).
- **Accountability** (spiritual radar checks).
- **Rest** (to avoid spiritual burnout).
- **Worship** (to reset your altitude and realign your focus).

Just like pilots run routine checks before every flight, you must keep checking your spiritual instruments.

In Full Flight

Ask yourself:

- Is my discernment sharp?
- Am I responding in obedience?
- Am I walking in peace or pressure?
- Am I in step with the Spirit or rushing ahead?

Without these check-ins, even seasoned eagles drift.

Galatians 5:25 says, *"If we live in the Spirit, let us also walk in the Spirit."*

DON'T FLY ALONE

The skies are wide. The journey is high. And the assignment is weighty. But you were never meant to navigate it alone.

The Holy Spirit is not only with you—He is **in you**. Guiding. Empowering. Lifting. Reminding you that no matter how heavy the storm or how thick the clouds—**He is your wind.**

So tune in.
Stay aligned.

And let the wind of heaven carry you higher than you ever imagined.

DON'T FLY IN SOMEONE ELSE'S PATTERN—FLY IN YOUR OWN

Every eagle has a unique flight pattern. Their wingspan, strength, instincts, and rhythm are distinct. Likewise, your spiritual journey, calling, and destiny are not meant to mirror anyone else's. Trying to copy another's pattern will not only wear you out—it will rob you of the freedom and fruitfulness of flying in your own.

YOU WERE DESIGNED UNIQUELY

Psalm 139:14 declares, *"I will praise thee; for I am fearfully and wonderfully made: marvellous are thy works; and that my soul knoweth right well."* That means your voice, gift, timing, and assignment are unlike anyone else's. God does not make duplicates—He makes originals.

Eli, the Young Eagle, once tried to imitate Zara's flying pattern but quickly found himself exhausted. Obed smiled and said, *"Her wings aren't your wings, Eli. Find your flow."*

COMPARISON CLOUDS CLARITY

When you focus on someone else's pattern, you lose sight of your own. 2 Corinthians 10:12 warns that comparing ourselves among ourselves is unwise. What's right for them may not be right for you. What elevates them may exhaust you.

Zara soared because she flew with confidence in her own God-given design. Her secret? She stayed in her lane and followed God's voice, not people's applause.

IMITATION LIMITS INNOVATION

You were created to reveal something new about God's glory. But when you copy others, you cover your own uniqueness. Romans 12:6 reminds us that we all have different gifts according to the grace given us. Imitation may gain attention, but it cannot unlock anointing.

Obed said, *"The sky is big enough for all of us. You don't need their path—you need your purpose."*

GOD BREATHES ON THE AUTHENTIC

There is grace for your pattern. When you move authentically in what God assigned to you, heaven backs you. Doors open, peace follows, and impact multiplies. Ephesians 2:10 says you are God's workmanship, created in Christ Jesus to do good works He prepared for you to do—not someone else.

When you try to soar in someone else's pattern, you will either fall or fly unfulfilled. But when you stay true to your pattern, you soar in purpose.

YOUR PATTERN IS PART OF THE GREATER PICTURE

Even in uniqueness, you are connected to a greater body. Your pattern contributes to the larger movement of the kingdom. You don't have to match others to matter. Like a flock that flies in formation, each eagle has a place—but flies in their own rhythm.

Pastor Dr. Claudine Benjamin

LET GO OF THE PRESSURE TO PERFORM

In a world of comparison and perfectionism, it is tempting to perform instead of soar. But you don't have to prove your value—you only need to live it. Galatians 1:10 asks, *"For do I now persuade men, or God? or do I seek to please men?"* Fly for His approval alone.

The most powerful version of you is the real one—the one God made, redeemed, and equipped.

REFLECTION QUESTIONS

- Have you been trying to fly in someone else's pattern?
- What unique qualities, gifts, and insights has God given you?
- How can you return to the authenticity of your own God-designed path?

DECLARATION

"I release comparison. I choose authenticity. I will no longer fly in someone else's pattern. I will soar in the rhythm God wrote for me, with the grace, gifts, and calling He designed just for me. I am original. I am anointed. I am aligned with heaven's plan for my life."

PRAYER

Lord, thank You for the spiritual tools You've given me to stay on course. Help me to navigate with wisdom, discernment, and truth. Just as an eagle adjusts its wings in flight, teach me how to adjust my spirit to stay aligned with You. Keep my heart tuned to heaven and my spirit maintained in Your Word and presence.

Scripture: Psalm 119:105 – *"Thy word is a lamp unto my feet, and a light unto my path."*

CHAPTER 9

I'M ANOINTED TO SOAR LIKE AN EAGLE

RISING BY DESIGN, EMPOWERED BY GOD

You weren't just born to fly—you were anointed to soar.

There is a divine difference between having wings and knowing how to use them. The eagle was not merely built for the sky—it was destined for it. Likewise, you weren't created to crawl through life hoping to survive. You were anointed to live above limits, discouragement, distraction, and defeat. You were equipped by God to rise into your divine destiny with power, poise, and prophetic purpose.

When God places His hand on your life, your flight is not optional—it's inevitable.

ANOINTED MEANS APPOINTED

The word "anointed" doesn't just mean chosen—it means empowered. When God anoints someone, He gives them the authority and strength to complete a divine assignment. And your assignment includes elevation.

Pastor Dr. Claudine Benjamin

You are anointed to:

- Rise above average.
- Live with supernatural perspective.
- Overcome adversity.
- Shift atmospheres.
- Lead with vision and boldness.
- Break generational curses.
- Fly in places others only dream about.

Just like the eagle is drawn toward the sky, your spirit is drawn toward destiny. You may feel fear, but fear is not your compass. Faith is.

Flight Insight: If God called you to it, He has empowered you for it.

RISING THROUGH RESISTANCE

Every eagle learns to fly through resistance. Its wings are strengthened not by ease but by the challenge of air pressure. The eagle leans into the wind to gain elevation.

So it is in your life. Every storm you've faced, every trial, every obstacle has strengthened your wings. Your anointing doesn't eliminate resistance—it gives you power to rise through it.

Joseph was anointed in a pit, refined in a prison, and exalted in a palace.

80

David was anointed as king but had to dodge spears and survive caves before he ever sat on the throne.

Jesus was filled with the Spirit but immediately led into the wilderness before launching His ministry.

Your resistance is not a rejection—it's your refinement. The oil of your anointing is pressed out in private before it is revealed in public.

Flight Insight: What you're going through is preparing you for where you're going to.

THE EAGLE'S VIEW: YOU SEE DIFFERENTLY

One of the most powerful traits of the eagle is its vision. It can see clearly for miles. When you are anointed to soar, you don't just go higher—you begin to see differently. You stop reacting to ground-level noise and start responding to heaven's voice.

Your vision becomes sharper. You're no longer driven by emotion—you're guided by revelation.

— When others panic, you perceive.
— When others retreat, you rise.
— When others conform, you transform.

The anointing doesn't just elevate your flight—it sharpens your focus.

Pastor Dr. Claudine Benjamin

Isaiah 40:31 says, *"But they that wait upon the Lord shall renew their strength; they shall mount up with wings as eagles; they shall run, and not be weary; and they shall walk, and not faint."*

This isn't a poetic line—it's a prophetic reality. When God renews your strength, He doesn't put you back where you were. He lifts you higher.

Flight Insight: Your anointing is not for popularity—it's for perspective.

SOARING ABOVE THE STORM

When storms come, most birds seek shelter. But the eagle doesn't run—it rises. It uses the power of the storm to lift it above the clouds.

You are not anointed to run from trouble—you're anointed to rise above it.

Your spiritual DNA is built for higher places. You don't avoid the storm—you overcome it. You don't deny the wind—you use it. That's what it means to soar under the anointing.

— Depression may knock—but it won't define you.
— Setbacks may slow you—but they won't stop you.
— Disappointments may sting—but they won't ground you.

You are anointed to soar above it all. Not in pride but in power. Not by performance but by the Spirit.

82

Flight Insight: When the enemy tries to ground you, remember—you were never built for the nest.

FLY WITH CONFIDENCE: YOU'RE EMPOWERED FOR THIS

You're not an eagle by accident. You're not anointed by accident. God chose you. He called you. He clothed you in grace. He empowered you by His Spirit.

It's time to:

- Own your calling.
- Embrace your identity.
- Activate your authority.
- Trust the wind of the Holy Spirit.
- Spread your wings and fly.

You were made for the high places. You were made for divine heights. This is not just a motivational phrase—it's a spiritual decree: You are anointed to soar.

YOUR FLIGHT IS A PROPHETIC ACT

When you rise, you make a prophetic statement: God is still lifting, still calling, still moving through His people. Your soaring life is a testimony that grace wins, faith works, and purpose still speaks.

So lift your head. Stretch your wings. And let the wind of the Spirit carry you. You were never meant to blend in with the chickens. You were born, chosen, and anointed—to fly like an eagle.

Pastor Dr. Claudine Benjamin

DECLARATIONS

"I declare that I'm anointed to soar."
Speak these aloud daily to align your spirit with your calling:

1. I am anointed to soar above fear, doubt, and limitation.

2. I was created for high places—mediocrity is not my portion.

3. I will rise with purpose, power, and prophetic vision.

4. I do not fear the storm—God uses it to lift me higher.

6. My setbacks are setups for a greater ascent.

7. I trust the wind of the Holy Spirit to carry me where I cannot go alone.

8. I break free from ground-level thinking and rise with kingdom perspective.

9. I am not alone—I fly with divine empowerment and favor.

10. I release the weight of yesterday so I can rise into tomorrow.

11. I am bold, chosen, equipped, and empowered. I am anointed to soar like an eagle.

In Full Flight

PRAYER

Father, in the name of Jesus, thank You for calling me higher. You didn't create me to crawl through life—you designed me to soar. I embrace the anointing You have placed on my life. I receive fresh wind from Your Spirit to rise above the noise, fear, weight, and distractions. Strengthen my wings. Sharpen my vision. Position my heart. Let me not flap in my own effort but trust in Your divine current to carry me. Let my life be a reflection of Your power, not my perfection.

I declare that my storms will not define me—they will elevate me. My faith will lift me. My obedience will align me. And my worship will keep me soaring. Use my flight to inspire others and give You glory. In Jesus' name. Amen.

SCRIPTURES AND REFLECTION

Meditate on these scriptures throughout the week.

"But they that wait upon the Lord shall renew their strength; they shall mount up with wings as eagles; they shall run, and not be weary; and they shall walk, and not faint." —Isaiah 40:31 - KJV

"He makes me as surefooted as a deer, enabling me to stand on mountain heights." —Psalm 18:33 - NLT

"Like an eagle that rouses her chicks and hovers over her young, so he spread his wings to take them up and carried them safely on his pinions. The Lord alone guided them; they followed no foreign gods." —Deuteronomy 32:11-12 - NLT

85

Pastor Dr. Claudine Benjamin

*"I press toward the mark for the prize of the high calling of God in Christ Jesus." —**Philippians 3:14 - KJV***

*"If the Spirit of him who raised Jesus from the dead dwells in you, he who raised Christ Jesus from the dead will also give life to your mortal bodies through his Spirit who dwells in you." —**Romans 8:11 - ESV***

CHAPTER 10

THE EAGLES AMONG US

UNDERSTANDING THE DIFFERENT TYPES OF EAGLES AND THEIR DIVINE FUNCTIONS

In the vast sky of divine purpose, no two eagles soar the same way. Just as God has uniquely designed natural eagles to fulfill specific functions in the ecosystem, He has crafted His children with different spiritual callings, personalities, and processes. The body of Christ is not a one-size-fits-all assembly—we are a majestic gathering of eagles, each with unique flight patterns, altitudes, and assignments.

Some are born to see far ahead. Others to battle in prayer. Some glide in divine rest while others rise again from brokenness. Together, we represent the full anatomy of a kingdom in motion.

Pastor Dr. Claudine Benjamin

MEET THE EAGLES: THE SYMBOLIC JOURNEY OF ELI, ZARA, AND OBED

ELI – THE REBUILDING EAGLE BECOMING A WARRIOR

Eli is young, full of questions, and still learning how to trust his wings. He represents those in transition—believers who have discovered their spiritual potential but are still finding the confidence to launch. Eli has not yet learned how to soar consistently; fear, self-doubt, and comparison often cloud his altitude.

He is currently in his molting stage, shedding insecurity, immature ambition, and the need for validation. But within him is a fierce heart—a warrior in the making. His moments of hesitation are balanced by his willingness to listen, learn, and try again.

Eli reminds us that great warriors are not born overnight. They are rebuilt in hidden places.

Spiritual Type: Rebuilding eagle, developing into warrior eagle.

Flight Strength: Teachable spirit, humble heart, resilience through mentorship.

Key Lesson: You don't have to fly perfectly—you just have to keep flapping.

ZARA – THE SOARING EAGLE WITH VISIONARY INSIGHT

Zara is majestic in the sky. Her flight is smooth, her vision is sharp, and her movements are purposeful. She doesn't flap wildly—she waits on the wind. Zara is not just a seasoned flier; she's in sync with the rhythms of heaven. She knows when to glide, when to rise, and when to rest.

She represents mature believers who have learned how to let God carry them. Her strength isn't just in her wings but in her wisdom. She sees what others miss, not because she's better—but because she's surrendered. Her altitude is the result of deep trust.

Zara mentors from above but never looks down on those still learning. She encourages Eli not to mimic her flight but to discover his own. Her life is proof that you can go far when you stop trying to control the wind and start partnering with it.

Zara reminds us that it's not about flapping harder—it's about trusting deeper.

Spiritual Type: Soaring eagle with visionary traits.

Flight Strength: Discernment, rest, and supernatural trust.

Key Lesson: True maturity is knowing when to fly, when to glide, and when to wait.

Pastor Dr. Claudine Benjamin

OBED – THE WEATHERED AND TEACHING EAGLE

Obed's feathers are worn, and his wings bear the evidence of battle. He has flown through storms that others didn't survive. There are scars under his wings—some physical, some emotional, all spiritual. But he still flies.

He represents the faithful fathers and mothers of the faith—those who have been broken but not beaten, wounded but not wasted. He is not just a survivor; he is a teacher. Every turbulence he overcame has become a lesson for someone else's flight.

Obed doesn't envy youth, nor does he rush wisdom. He knows the value of endurance and the power of stillness. He speaks little, but when he does, the young eagles listen. He doesn't boast of his journey—he simply shares it.

Obed reminds us that your scars don't ground you—they guide others.

Spiritual Type: Weathered eagle with teaching traits.

Flight Strength: Wisdom, endurance, and quiet authority.

Key Lesson: You can still soar after the storm.

EAGLES AND SPIRITUAL FUNCTION

Here are some scriptures that align with the spiritual symbolism and eagle types in this chapter.

Eagles in Scripture:

"But they that wait upon the Lord shall renew their strength; they shall mount up with wings as eagles; they shall run, and not be weary; and they shall walk, and not faint." —Isaiah 40:31

"As an eagle stirreth up her nest, fluttereth over her young, spreadeth abroad her wings, taketh them, beareth them on her wings: So the Lord alone did lead him, and there was no strange god with him." —Deuteronomy 32:11-12

" Doth the eagle mount up at thy command, and make her nest on high? She dwelleth and abideth on the rock, upon the crag of the rock, and the strong place. From thence she seeketh the prey, and her eyes behold afar off." —Job 39:27-29

Visionary Eagle:

"I will stand upon my watch, and set me upon the tower, and will watch to see what he will say unto me, and what I shall answer when I am reproved. And the Lord answered me, and said, Write the vision, and make it plain upon tables, that he may run that readeth it. For the vision is yet for an appointed time, but at the end it shall speak, and not lie: though it tarry, wait for it; because it will surely come, it will not tarry." —Habakkuk 2:1-3

"Where there is no vision, the people perish: but he that keepeth the law, happy is he." —Proverbs 29:18

Warrior Eagle:

"For we wrestle not against flesh and blood, but against principalities, against powers, against the rulers of the darkness of

Pastor Dr. Claudine Benjamin

this world, against spiritual wickedness in high places. Wherefore take unto you the whole armour of God, that ye may be able to withstand in the evil day, and having done all, to stand." — **Ephesians 6:12-13**

"(For the weapons of our warfare are not carnal, but mighty through God to the pulling down of strong holds;)" —2 **Corinthians 10:4**

Soaring Eagle:

*"Rest in the Lord, and wait patiently for him: fret not thyself because of him who prospereth in his way, because of the man who bringeth wicked devices to pass." —***Psalm 37:7**

*"Ye have seen what I did unto the Egyptians, and how I bare you on eagles' wings, and brought you unto myself." —***Exodus 19:4**

Teaching Eagle:

*"And the things that thou hast heard of me among many witnesses, the same commit thou to faithful men, who shall be able to teach others also." —***2 Timothy 2:2**

*"Wisdom is the principal thing; therefore get wisdom: and with all thy getting get understanding." —***Proverbs 4:7**

Weathered Eagle:

*"Blessed is the man that endureth temptation: for when he is tried, he shall receive the crown of life, which the Lord hath promised to them that love him." —***James 1:12**

"We are troubled on every side, yet not distressed; we are perplexed, but not in despair; Persecuted, but not forsaken; cast down, but not destroyed;" —**2 Corinthians 4:8-9**

Rebuilding Eagle:

"Create in me a clean heart, O God; and renew a right spirit within me. Cast me not away from thy presence; and take not thy holy spirit from me. Restore unto me the joy of thy salvation; and uphold me with thy free spirit." —**Psalm 51:10-12**

"To appoint unto them that mourn in Zion, to give unto them beauty for ashes, the oil of joy for mourning, the garment of praise for the spirit of heaviness; that they might be called trees of righteousness, the planting of the Lord, that he might be glorified." —**Isaiah 61:3**

In the natural world, eagles come in many forms—each with unique traits, purposes, and patterns of flight. Spiritually, we too resemble different kinds of eagles, shaped by our experiences, callings, and roles in the kingdom. Not every eagle soars the same way, but each is necessary in God's divine sky.

Understanding the different types of eagles can help us recognize ourselves, honor the journey of others, and embrace the role we were designed to fulfill.

THE VISIONARY EAGLE – SEERS OF THE SKY

This eagle has unmatched vision. It sees what others can't and perceives danger before it arrives. Spiritually, the visionary eagle represents prophets, intercessors, dreamers, and discerners—those called to see into the future and warn, prepare, or direct the body of Christ.

Function: To watch, guard, and guide.

Strength: Clarity and foresight.

Warning: Isolation can blur discernment. Stay connected to the flock.

Flight Insight: If you're called to see far, stay close to the One who sees all.

THE WARRIOR EAGLE – FIERCE AND FEARLESS

This eagle is aggressive in battle, with strong talons and unmatched courage. It symbolizes spiritual warriors—those who are called to fight in prayer, confront injustice, and defend the vulnerable.

Function: To tear down strongholds and protect spiritual territory.

Strength: Boldness, authority, and anointing.

Warning: Don't mistake combat for identity. You are more than the fight.

Flight Insight: Warriors must know when to war and when to rest.

THE SOARING EAGLE – GRACEFUL IN PURPOSE

This eagle glides with minimal effort, carried by unseen currents of wind. The soaring eagle represents believers who have mastered

In Full Flight

trust in God's timing and strength. Their life is a testimony of grace, balance, and divine rhythm.

Function: To model rest, trust, and consistent elevation.

Strength: Wisdom, patience, and peace.

Warning: Don't become passive—soaring is not stagnation.

Flight Insight: You rise higher when you surrender to the Wind of the Spirit.

THE TEACHING EAGLE – DISCIPLER OF THE YOUNG

This eagle trains its young to fly, often pushing them from the nest to teach resilience. Spiritually, this eagle represents mentors, pastors, and teachers who develop the next generation of kingdom fliers.

Function: To teach, equip, and release.

Strength: Patience, compassion, and structure.

Warning: Don't carry what was meant to be pushed.

Flight Insight: Teaching is not just giving knowledge—it's creating launch pads.

THE WEATHERED EAGLE – SCARRED BUT STILL SOARING

This eagle has battle wounds and weathered feathers, but it still flies. It has survived storms, predators, and long flights. Spiritually, this eagle is the seasoned believer—the intercessor, elder, or leader who carries wisdom from survival.

Function: To counsel, comfort, and stabilize.

Strength: Endurance, humility, and experience.

Warning: Don't let past storms silence your current voice.

Flight Insight: Your scars don't ground you—they validate your strength.

THE REBUILDING EAGLE – RESTORER IN PROCESS

At times, eagles go through a molting season where they lose old feathers and grow new ones. During this phase, they look weak and grounded. Spiritually, this eagle represents those in healing, transition, or renewal.

Function: To rebuild identity, restore flight, and refresh purpose.

Strength: Surrender, faith, and renewal.

Warning: Don't confuse a pause with a disqualification.

Flight Insight: The ground is not your grave—it's your grooming place.

ONE SKY, MANY EAGLES

In God's kingdom, there is room in the sky for all types of eagles. You may be a visionary, warrior, teacher, or one in rebuilding—but your flight matters. Don't compare your wings to someone else's. Don't judge another eagle's flight pattern. Learn to honor your own process and help others embrace theirs.

Whether you're soaring, fighting, teaching, healing, or watching—just keep flying.

You were born for the sky.

CLOSING PRAYER

Lord, thank You for placing powerful eagles in my life—those who soar with You and encourage others to do the same. Let me be wise to recognize mentors, leaders, and fellow flyers You've sent to help me grow. And help me, in turn, to be an eagle that uplifts and empowers others on their own journey.

Scripture: Proverbs 27:17 – *"Iron sharpeneth iron; so a man sharpeneth the countenance of his friend."*

CHAPTER 11

THE EAGLE AND THE STORM

In the natural world, few creatures are as majestic and resilient as the eagle. With its powerful wingspan, keen vision, and commanding presence, the eagle is not only the king of the sky but also a living metaphor for strength, strategy, and spiritual endurance. When a storm arises, most birds seek shelter. They hide from the winds, rain, and lightning. But the eagle? The eagle does something entirely different: the eagle flies into the storm.

Rather than fleeing from the turbulence, the eagle locks its wings, embraces the powerful updrafts, and uses the storm to rise above it. The storm, which others fear, becomes the very vehicle that lifts the eagle to higher altitudes. The winds that were meant to buffet and break become the means of elevation.

So it is with the believer.

Life's storms—those moments of unexpected trials, painful losses, and overwhelming opposition—can either defeat us or define us. When we lean into the wind with our faith anchored in God, we discover strength we didn't know we had and a grace that carries us above the storm.

Pastor Dr. Claudine Benjamin

SPIRITUAL LESSONS FROM THE EAGLE

VISION IN THE STORM

The eagle has incredibly sharp vision and is able to spot its prey from miles away, even during turbulent conditions. Spiritually, this speaks of clarity in chaos. When we are grounded in the Word and led by the Spirit, storms don't blur our purpose—they sharpen it.

*"Where there is no vision, the people perish: but he that keepeth the law, happy is he." —**Proverbs 29:18***

*"I will instruct thee and teach thee in the way which thou shalt go: I will guide thee with mine eye." —**Psalm 32:8***

POSITIONING FOR ELEVATION

The eagle positions itself to catch the wind, not fight against it. Likewise, believers must position themselves in prayer, praise, and obedience, allowing the power of God to lift them above adversity.

*"But they that wait upon the Lord shall renew their strength; they shall mount up with wings as eagles; they shall run, and not be weary; and they shall walk, and not faint." —**Isaiah 40:31***

LONGEVITY THROUGH STORMS

Eagles are known for their longevity and their ability to renew themselves. In the middle of your storm, God is not just helping you survive; He is preparing you to thrive. Your storm is not your end—it's your setup for renewal.

"For which cause we faint not; but though our outward man perish, yet the inward man is renewed day by day." —**2 Corinthians 4:16**

REFLECTION

— What storm are you currently facing, and how are you responding?

— Are you hiding from the winds or positioning yourself to rise above them?

——What would it look like for you to "fly into the storm" with faith this week?

PRAYER

Mighty God, thank You for being my refuge in every storm. Just as the eagle uses the storm's wind to rise higher, help me to turn trials into triumphs. Teach me to see storms not as setbacks but as setups for elevation. Let my faith increase, my vision sharpen, and my heart remain steadfast as You carry me through every gust and thunder.

Scripture: Nahum 1:7 – *"The Lord is good, a strong hold in the day of trouble; and he knoweth them that trust in him."*

CHAPTER 12

WHEN THE EAGLE LOSES ITS FEATHERS

*"Who satisfieth thy mouth with good things; so that thy youth is renewed like the eagle's." —**Psalm 103:5***

There comes a season in the life of every eagle—a defining moment of weakness, vulnerability, and deep transformation. This season is known as molting. It is a painful, lonely process in which the eagle begins to lose its feathers, and in doing so, it loses its ability to fly, hunt, and soar in the skies as it once did. For a time, the king of the skies becomes grounded.

To the untrained eye, the molting eagle appears to be dying. Its once sharp beak becomes brittle and curved. Its talons—symbols of power and precision—begin to lose their strength. The feathers fall out, one by one, leaving bare spots and exposing the eagle to harsh winds and sunlight. It cannot fly. It cannot hunt. It cannot defend itself. It retreats to a solitary, high place, hidden from the world.

THE PLACE OF ISOLATION AND REFLECTION

This image of the molting eagle is a powerful metaphor for the spiritual process many of us face. There are times in life when God allows us to be stripped—of our strength, comfort, roles, and routines. Just as the eagle hides in the mountains, we too are drawn into seasons of isolation—not for punishment, but for purpose.

This is the process after the storm. When the winds die down, the loss becomes visible. You're not the same. You feel exposed, unsure, and worn out. But hear this: God is not finished with you. You are not broken beyond repair. You are simply in the sacred process of being renewed.

In this place of solitude, the eagle begins the painful task of restoration. It breaks off its old beak by striking it against a rock. It pulls out its talons. Why? Because the old cannot serve the new. The old tools, the old methods, the old weapons—it all has to go. This is the part of the process we resist the most: letting go. But unless we surrender the old, we will never receive the new.

STRIPPED BUT NOT DEFEATED

You may feel like you've lost everything. You may be wondering, *"Where is God in all of this?"* He's with you—in the hiding place, in the breaking, in the process. He is allowing you to be emptied so He can refill you.

Psalm 91:1 reminds us, *"He that dwelleth in the secret place of the most High shall abide under the shadow of the Almighty."* The molting eagle hides in the cleft of the rock, and so must you. When you are under the shadow of God, even your weakest season becomes a womb for greatness.

Isaiah 40:29-31 beautifully captures this process: *"He giveth power to the faint; and to them that have no might he increaseth strength. Even the youths shall faint and be weary, and the young men shall utterly fall: But they that wait upon the Lord shall renew their strength; they shall mount up with wings as eagles; they shall run, and not be weary; and they shall walk, and not faint."*

This promise wasn't written for the strong but for the weary. It was written for the one who feels grounded, forgotten, and tired of waiting. Your strength is coming back. Your wings are being restored. The storm may have grounded you, but the process will cause you to soar again.

NEW FEATHERS, NEW ALTITUDE

As the eagle waits, something miraculous happens. Slowly, new feathers begin to grow. Stronger. Lighter. Sleeker. The beak grows back, sharper than before. The talons regenerate with renewed grip. And, one day, the eagle opens its wings and feels the wind once again. It launches from the mountain and soars higher than it did before, not just because it has new feathers—but because it has survived the process.

That's what God is doing in you. He is not just healing you. He is transforming you. You will not only recover from this storm, but you will rise from it with new vision, new strength, and a deeper trust in God than ever before.

There comes a time in the eagle's life when it begins to lose its feathers. This season is called molting, a natural and necessary process that looks like weakness but leads to power. During molting, the eagle's vision dims, its beak grows brittle, and its feathers fall out. This once-powerful bird now finds itself grounded, vulnerable, and alone.

105

Pastor Dr. Claudine Benjamin

Many believers find themselves in this same place—a season of spiritual molting—a place where strength seems lost, where the soaring of past victories feels like a distant memory. You may feel grounded, even forgotten. Your praise may feel weaker, your prayer life quieter, your purpose clouded. But don't mistake the process for defeat.

THE MOLTING PLACE: A VALLEY OF RENEWAL

The eagle retreats to a high, isolated mountain during this phase. There, it beats its beak against the rock to break the old and allow the new to grow. It plucks out weakened talons and waits—helpless but hopeful.

Spiritually, this is symbolic of our retreat to God, our Rock. In this molting season, God often strips away what we rely on—relationships, platforms, titles, and even habits. He allows us to experience brokenness so that His healing can take root.

Psalm 103:5 says, *"Who satisfieth thy mouth with good things; so that thy youth is renewed like the eagle's."* This isn't poetic fluff—it's a promise. God doesn't leave you in the molting. He uses it.

WHEN NEW FEATHERS GROW

In time, the eagle's strength returns. New feathers replace the old. Its vision is sharpened. Its beak and talons grow back stronger than before. The eagle takes flight again—this time with greater endurance, renewed strength, and deeper wisdom.

In Full Flight

What you thought was your breaking point was God's renewal point. You may feel grounded, but you're just in hiding for healing. When you come out, you'll soar higher than before.

WHAT TO REMEMBER IN THE MOLTING SEASON

1. You are not alone. God is with you in your isolation.

2. This is temporary. Molting doesn't last forever—it's a season.

3. You are being renewed, not rejected. What feels like loss is actually preparation.

4. Your next flight will be your highest yet. Don't rush the process.

REFLECTION QUESTIONS

1. What "old feathers" (habits, relationships, beliefs) might God be asking you to release?

2. How can you dwell in the "secret place" and draw closer to God during this season?

3. What new things do you believe God wants to birth in you after this process?

Pastor Dr. Claudine Benjamin

PRAYER

Lord, in seasons of loss and renewal, remind me that You are doing a deeper work in me. Even when I feel stripped and weak, You are preparing me for a stronger comeback. Help me not to fear the molting process, but to embrace it as a necessary step for transformation and renewed strength.

Scripture: Job 23:10 – *"But he knoweth the way that I take: when he hath tried me, I shall come forth as gold."*

CHAPTER 13

WHEN YOU ARE IN FULL FLIGHT— NATURALLY AND SPIRITUALLY

There are seasons in life when everything aligns. The wind is at your back, the path is clear, and momentum is on your side. You are soaring—naturally and spiritually. These are the moments when prayers are answered quickly, doors open effortlessly, and the purpose God placed within you feels tangible and alive.

NATURALLY IN FLIGHT

In the natural, being in full flight may look like progress, promotion, stability, and favor. It's when your gifts make room for you; what you've worked for begins to flourish. This season brings joy, excitement, and a sense of accomplishment. But it also brings responsibility. When you are elevated, more eyes are watching, more is expected, and your choices carry greater weight.

It is easy to become comfortable in the momentum. But full flight doesn't mean autopilot. Even eagles, which are born to soar, must remain alert in the skies. Distractions, storms, and predators don't disappear just because you're flying high.

109

Pastor Dr. Claudine Benjamin

SPIRITUALLY IN FLIGHT

Spiritually, full flight is a place of deep connection with God. Your prayer life is vibrant, your faith is strong, and your spiritual ears are open to His voice. You are walking in obedience, discerning His will, and seeing the fruit of your labor in the kingdom.

This is where revelation flows easily, worship is pure, and your service to others is fruitful. But this level of spiritual flight comes with warfare. The higher you go, the thinner the air. The enemy does not attack those who are idle—he targets those in motion, especially those soaring toward purpose.

Full flight is not just about height, but about divine strength and direction. When God lifts you, no man can bring you down unless you surrender your wings.

THE BALANCE OF FLIGHT

To fly in both realms—natural and spiritual—is to walk in balance. It requires humility to stay grounded in character while ascending in influence. It demands constant prayer to remain aligned with God's timing, lest you fly ahead of His plan. And it requires discernment because not every open sky is safe to soar.

When you're in full flight, never forget Who gave you wings. Guard your heart, steward your platform, and keep your eyes on the Lord. The goal is not just to rise but to remain in His will while you do.

REFLECTION

1. Are you currently in a season of full flight or preparing to take off?

2. How are you stewarding this season—both naturally and spiritually?

3. Are you alert to the subtle distractions that can arise in high places?

There comes a point in the journey when all the waiting, labor, and tears begin to make sense. You rise, not by accident, not by chance, but by divine design. This is the season when you are in full flight—soaring high, both in the natural and the spiritual. It is the manifestation of God's promises in your life, the fulfillment of prophetic words, the reward of obedience, and the evidence that you are walking in alignment with His will.

THE POWER OF MOMENTUM

Momentum is a gift. In the natural, it feels like everything is finally working. The job you prayed for, the business you built, the family you dreamed of—it all begins to flourish. You're not just surviving; you're thriving. But with momentum comes motion, and with motion comes exposure. You are no longer hidden. Your name is being mentioned in rooms you have never entered. Your influence is growing, and with that comes the need for greater wisdom, character, and discernment.

Don't confuse movement with maturity. Just because you're flying doesn't mean you're invincible. Even aircrafts at cruising altitude still require navigation, regular checks, and communication with control towers. The same is true in life—no matter how high you soar, you must stay connected to your Source.

SPIRITUAL ALTITUDE: SOARING WITH GOD

Spiritually, being in full flight means you are operating in your anointing. Your sensitivity to the Holy Spirit is sharp. Your worship is pure, your vision is clear, and your heart is in sync with heaven. You are producing spiritual fruit. You are effective in ministry, prayer, intercession, and leadership. You are walking in the overflow.

But even in this place of spiritual success, humility is your lifeline. **Lucifer once flew high in heavenly realms, but pride brought him down.** Flight without humility is dangerous. The higher God elevates you, the lower you must bow. Keep your spirit anchored in prayer and your motives purified by the fire of God's presence.

THE EAGLE'S PERSPECTIVE

The Bible often compares the believer to an eagle. Eagles soar higher than any other bird, but they also fly alone. Not everyone can go where you're going. Some people are only equipped for low altitudes. Don't be surprised when old relationships fall away in this season. Your vision is too great, your assignment too weighty to be distracted by people who don't understand the altitude you're called to maintain.

Eagles use the wind of the storm to rise higher. Similarly, God often uses adversity to elevate His people. What tried to break you only helped you ascend. What the enemy meant for evil, God used to lift you.

THE DISCIPLINE OF SUSTAINED FLIGHT

It's one thing to take off and another thing entirely to stay in the air. The weight of success, the pressure of visibility, the demands of leadership—these things can be exhausting. You must learn the art of rest in motion. You must know when to retreat, when to recharge, and when to say no. **Sustained flight requires structure.**

— Stay in the Word.
— Stay in worship.
— Stay accountable.
— Stay teachable.

When Elijah was in full prophetic flight, calling down fire and performing miracles, he still had a moment when he crashed from exhaustion. God had to call him aside, feed him, and restore him. Never be so anointed that you neglect your humanity. Your spirit may soar, but your body needs care.

A HIGHER CALLING, A HEAVIER RESPONSIBILITY

To whom much is given, much is required (see Luke 12:48). Flight is not for show—it is for purpose. God did not elevate you just to say He could. He lifted you so you could see further, reach further, and impact more. You are now a carrier of light, a representative of

113

Pastor Dr. Claudine Benjamin

the kingdom. Your testimony matters. Your integrity matters. Your obedience matters.

You can no longer afford to act on emotion. You can no longer afford spiritual complacency. The people connected to your flight are depending on your stability. They are watching your altitude. Don't descend to respond to distractions. Stay focused. Stay faithful.

WHEN THE WIND CHANGES

Every flyer must be prepared for turbulence. Seasons shift. Winds change. What once was easy may now become difficult. But remember: your wings are built for this. God did not give you flight just to show you the sky—He gave you flight to conquer it.

Even when the wind turns against you, **He is your lift.** When people change, when favor seems to fade, when trials come back to test your wings—stay the course. You are not flying alone. God is the wind beneath you, the compass guiding you, and the net that will catch you if you fall.

REFLECTION QUESTIONS

1. Are you currently in a season of spiritual and natural momentum?

2. How are you maintaining humility in this season of elevation?

3. What habits and disciplines do you need to strengthen to sustain this level of flight?

4. Have you created enough space for rest, reflection, and realignment with God?

PRAYER

Father, thank You for aligning my natural and spiritual life. Help me to soar in both realms with grace, wisdom, and power. Let my full flight reflect Your glory and Your plan. May I be fully yielded to Your Spirit so that every area of my life flows with divine purpose.

Scripture: 3 John 1:2 – *"Beloved, I wish above all things that thou mayest prosper and be in health, even as thy soul prospereth."*

CHAPTER 14

WHAT CAUSES THE PLANE TO FLY HIGH - WITH SPIRITUAL INSIGHTS

From the ground, watching a massive airplane soar across the sky can feel like witnessing a miracle. How does something so heavy, built of metal, with hundreds of passengers, fly high above the clouds as if it weighs nothing at all? The answer lies in the incredible combination of science, engineering, and the principles of flight.

THE FOUR FORCES OF FLIGHT

To understand what makes a plane fly high, we need to look at the four main forces that act on an aircraft when it is in the sky: Lift, Weight, Thrust, and Drag.

LIFT

Lift is the upward force that pushes the plane into the sky. It is created by the wings. The wings are specially designed in a shape called an airfoil, which causes air to move faster over the top of the wing and slower underneath. This difference in air pressure creates lift. The faster a plane moves forward, the more air flows over the wings and the greater the lift.

WEIGHT

Weight is the force of gravity pulling the plane downward. It's the total mass of the airplane, including passengers, fuel, cargo, and the plane itself. For the plane to go up, lift must be greater than weight. This balance is crucial. Pilots and engineers carefully calculate how much weight the plane can carry to ensure it can still lift off and fly high.

THRUST

Thrust is the forward force that moves the airplane ahead. It's generated by the plane's engines, either jet engines or propellers. Thrust allows the airplane to gain speed along the runway and eventually take off. Once in the air, continuous thrust helps the plane maintain or increase altitude.

DRAG

Drag is the resistance the plane experiences as it moves through the air—like wind pushing against your hand when you stick it out of a car window. Engineers design planes to be aerodynamic, meaning smooth and sleek, to reduce drag and allow the plane to cut through the air efficiently.

CLIMBING HIGHER INTO THE SKY

Once the plane is in the air, climbing higher depends on increasing lift and maintaining the right angle. Pilots adjust the angle of attack, which is the angle between the wing and the oncoming air. If it's too steep, the plane could stall. But at the right angle, the plane continues to climb.

As the plane rises, the air becomes thinner. That's why there's a limit to how high most planes can fly. Commercial jets usually cruise between 30,000 to 40,000 feet, where the air is thin enough to reduce drag but thick enough to still provide lift and oxygen for engines.

THE ROLE OF JET ENGINES

Jet engines are powerful machines. They suck in air, compress it, mix it with fuel, ignite it, and shoot it out the back at high speeds. This reaction produces the thrust needed for the plane to fly forward. As the plane gains speed, the wings generate more lift, allowing the plane to ascend.

CABIN PRESSURE AND HIGH ALTITUDES

Flying high has its advantages—less turbulence, better fuel efficiency, and faster travel. But humans can't survive without oxygen at high altitudes. That's why planes are pressurized. The cabin is sealed, and air is pumped in to create a livable environment at cruising altitudes.

THE FLIGHT INSTRUMENTS AND CONTROLS

Pilots rely on instruments to monitor altitude, speed, and engine performance. They use the elevator, rudder, and ailerons to control the direction and stability of the plane. When a pilot wants to climb, they raise the nose of the aircraft using the elevator, increasing lift.

Pastor Dr. Claudine Benjamin

WHY PLANES DON'T FALL FROM THE SKY

As long as the engines are running and the plane is properly controlled, it remains in the air because of the balance of the four forces. Even if an engine fails, modern planes are designed to glide safely. Pilots are trained for such emergencies and can still control the descent and landing.

WHAT CAUSES THE PLANE TO FLY HIGH?

(SPIRITUAL INSIGHT)

In the natural, a plane flies high due to four main principles: **lift, thrust, drag, and weight.** These forces work together to elevate and sustain flight. Spiritually, the believer's ability to **"fly high"** or rise above life's challenges depends on a divine set of forces at work in the life led by purpose and the Spirit of God.

LIFT – FAITH AND FAVOR

Lift in aviation is generated by the wings and airflow. Spiritually, **faith is your lift.** It positions you to rise above fear, doubt, and earthly limitations. Favor, the unearned grace of God, gives you access to places beyond your natural reach.

"But without faith it is impossible to please him: for he that cometh to God must believe that he is, and that he is a rewarder of them that diligently seek him." —Hebrews 11:6

"For thou, Lord, wilt bless the righteous; with favour wilt thou compass him as with a shield." —Psalm 5:12

120

Faith activates altitude. Favor sustains it.

THRUST – PURPOSE AND PASSION

Thrust is the forward-moving power that pushes the aircraft ahead. **Purpose is your spiritual thrust.** When you discover your why, it gives power to your what. **Passion** fuels that purpose with intensity and direction.

"Then I said, I will not make mention of him, nor speak any more in his name. But his word was in mine heart as a burning fire shut up in my bones, and I was weary with forbearing, and I could not stay." —Philippians 3:14

"...His word is in my heart like a fire, a fire shut up in my bones..." —Jeremiah 20:9

Without thrust, there is no forward movement—just stagnation.

DRAG – RESISTANCE AND REFINEMENT

Drag in the natural slows down the plane. Spiritually, **drag represents resistance—trials, opposition, or delays.** While uncomfortable, drag has a purpose. It refines your character and keeps you from crashing due to pride or unbalanced acceleration.

"My brethren, count it all joy when ye fall into divers temptations; Knowing this, that the trying of your faith worketh patience. But let patience have her perfect work, that ye may be perfect and entire, wanting nothing." —James 1:2-4

Pastor Dr. Claudine Benjamin

"And not only so, but we glory in tribulations also: knowing that tribulation worketh patience; And patience, experience; and experience, hope:" —**Romans 5:3-4**

Resistance builds resilience. Drag is a necessary tension.

WEIGHT – HUMILITY AND DEPENDENCE ON GOD

Weight is what keeps the plane grounded during rest and helps it balance in the air. Spiritually, **humility and total dependence on God** serve as the right "weight" to keep us grounded in character while still ascending in calling.

"Humble yourselves therefore under the mighty hand of God, that he may exalt you in due time:" —*1 Peter 5:6*

"Trust in the Lord with all thine heart; and lean not unto thine own understanding. In all thy ways acknowledge him, and he shall direct thy paths." —*Proverbs 3:5-6*

Too little weight (pride) causes instability. The right weight keeps you centered.

SPIRITUAL FLIGHT SUMMARY

- **Lift** = Faith and Favor
- **Thrust** = Purpose and Passion
- **Drag** = Resistance and Refinement
- **Weight** = Humility and Dependence

All of these working together allow the believer to fly high and **stay high**—above fear, distractions, and anything beneath your destiny.

122

PRAYER

Lord, show me the spiritual laws and disciplines that cause my life to rise in You. Help me to apply faith, prayer, fasting, and obedience so that I can ascend to the heights You've called me to. Let my flight be sustained by eternal truths.

Scripture: Isaiah 33:6 – *"And wisdom and knowledge shall be the stability of thy times, and strength of salvation: the fear of the Lord is his treasure."*

CHAPTER 15

WHAT DO WE NEED SPIRITUALLY TO FLY?

When we watch a plane rise into the sky, it's not only a technological marvel—it's a powerful spiritual metaphor. God did not create us to live in the valley of defeat or to remain grounded by fear, sin, or doubt. He created us to soar. But spiritual flight, like natural flight, requires alignment with divine laws and spiritual principles.

To spiritually take off and stay in the air, we need five essential elements: Faith, the Word of God, the Holy Spirit, Obedience, and Perseverance. These form the foundation of spiritual elevation and sustained progress in our walk with Christ.

FAITH – THE LIFT THAT ELEVATES US

"But they that wait upon the Lord shall renew their strength; they shall mount up with wings as eagles; they shall run, and not be weary; and they shall walk, and not faint." —**Isaiah 40:31**

Faith is the spiritual lift. Just as the wings of a plane are designed to create lift when moving through air, our faith catches the promises of God and elevates us above the limitations of this world.

Pastor Dr. Claudine Benjamin

Hebrews 11:6 says, *"without faith it is impossible to please Him..."* Faith is the starting point of flight. You cannot fly without believing that God has called you higher. Faith believes in the unseen, trusts in the impossible, and obeys without always having full understanding.

Faith gives us altitude.

It lifts us above:

- Fear (see 2 Timothy 1:7).
- Failure (see Micah 7:8).
- Frustration (see Philippians 4:6–7).

THE WORD OF GOD – THE ENGINE THAT PROPELS

"Thy word is a lamp unto my feet, and a light unto my path." — **Psalm 119:105**

A plane without engines cannot move forward—no matter how perfect its wings are. Likewise, believers without the Word cannot progress spiritually. The Word gives us clarity, vision, direction, and power.

Jesus declared in Matthew 4:4, *"Man shall not live by bread alone, but by every word that proceedeth out of the mouth of God."* The Word feeds your spirit and builds up your faith (see Romans 10:17). It teaches, corrects, trains, and equips (see 2 Timothy 3:16–17). The Word is both fuel and map.

Without the Word:

- We drift.
- We burn out.
- We lose our course.

With the Word:

- We move with purpose.
- We gain momentum.
- We arrive at God-ordained destinations.

THE HOLY SPIRIT – THE WIND BENEATH OUR WINGS

*"Not by might, nor by power, but by my spirit, saith the Lord of hosts." —**Zechariah 4:6***

Every pilot knows that air is essential for lift. Without air, wings are useless. In the same way, without the Holy Spirit, we cannot ascend spiritually. He is the Breath of God—the wind that gives us lift, guidance, and power.

Jesus told His disciples in John 16:13 that the Spirit would guide them into all truth. In Acts 1:8, He promised they would receive power when the Holy Spirit came upon them. The Holy Spirit gives us the ability to overcome sin, discern truth, minister effectively, and endure hardship.

Pastor Dr. Claudine Benjamin

The Holy Spirit empowers you to:

- Soar when you're tired.
- Glide when you don't understand.
- Navigate storms with wisdom.

He gives spiritual altitude even when life tries to push you down.

OBEDIENCE – THE CONTROL THAT STEERS US

"If ye be willing and obedient, ye shall eat the good of the land:"
—Isaiah 1:19

In an aircraft, the pilot must use precise controls to guide the plane. Even a small miscalculation can lead to disaster. Likewise, obedience is what keeps us aligned with God's direction. Disobedience may feel like freedom, but it quickly leads to chaos and crash landings.

Obedience means listening to the voice of the Lord and doing what He says—even when it's hard. Abraham obeyed God and left his homeland without knowing where he was going (see Hebrews 11:8). His obedience led to elevation.

Delayed obedience is disobedience. Partial obedience is disobedience.

Obedience will keep you:

- On course spiritually.
- Aligned with your purpose.
- Protected from unnecessary turbulence.

PERSEVERANCE – THE ENDURANCE TO STAY IN THE AIR

"Wherefore seeing we also are compassed about with so great a cloud of witnesses, let us lay aside every weight, and the sin which doth so easily beset us, and let us run with patience the race that is set before us, looking unto Jesus the author and finisher of our faith; who for the joy that was set before him endured the cross, despising the shame, and is set down at the right hand of the throne of God."
—Hebrews 12:1–2

A plane isn't successful just because it takes off—it must also stay in the air and reach its destination. Many believers start well but struggle with consistency. It's not about how high you fly at first but how well you endure the journey.

Life will test your perseverance. Storms will come. Wind resistance will increase. But perseverance keeps your spiritual wings stretched out, catching the wind of the Spirit even when your strength feels gone.

James 1:12 says, *"Blessed is the man that endureth temptation: for when he is tried, he shall receive the crown of life, which the Lord hath promised to them that love him."*

Perseverance means:

- Pushing when you feel like quitting.
- Praying when you don't see results.
- Praising through the pain.

Pastor Dr. Claudine Benjamin

THE LAWS OF SPIRITUAL FLIGHT

Here are some powerful takeaways for staying airborne spiritually:

- **Stay light** – *"Lay aside every weight..."* (see Hebrews 12:1). Sin and emotional baggage weigh us down.

- **Keep your eyes on Jesus** – *"Looking unto Jesus, the Author and Finisher..."* (see Hebrews 12:2). The pilot doesn't take their eyes off the sky. You shouldn't either.

- **Expect turbulence** – *"In this world you will have trouble..."* (see John 16:33). But God has already given you peace to fly through it.

- **Trust the process** – Every flight requires faith in the design. You were built to fly not crash.

YOU WERE BORN TO SOAR

God has already given you wings. The real question is—will you stretch them? Will you take the risk to fly in faith, powered by His Word, carried by His Spirit, guided by obedience, and strengthened by perseverance?

Your spiritual altitude is determined by your spiritual attitude. The higher you go, the clearer the vision, the quieter the noise, and the greater the freedom.

You were not created to crawl. You were designed to fly.

CHAPTER 16

DISTURBANCES IN FLIGHT AND HOW TO HANDLE THEM SUCCESSFULLY

Every pilot knows that no flight is ever perfectly smooth from takeoff to landing. Even the most advanced aircraft, flown by experienced pilots, encounter unexpected disturbances—turbulence, storms, wind shear, and more. These challenges are not signs of failure; they are a natural part of flight.

Likewise, in our spiritual journey, disturbances come. They shake our confidence, test our faith, and sometimes make us question whether we were ever meant to fly. But disturbances don't mean defeat—they're often indicators that you're in motion, in progress, and in purpose.

TYPES OF SPIRITUAL DISTURBANCES

TURBULENCE – UNSEEN BUT FELT

"We are troubled on every side, yet not distressed; we are perplexed, but not in despair;" —2 Corinthians 4:8

Turbulence in aviation is caused by sudden changes in wind. It can't always be seen, but it's deeply felt. Spiritually, turbulence shows

131

up as anxiety, emotional unrest, or unexpected resistance. You didn't see it coming, but it shakes your peace.

Spiritual turbulence includes:

- Conflict in relationships.
- Sudden disappointment.
- Inner spiritual battles.
- Seasons of confusion or fear.

Yet, planes are designed to withstand turbulence—and so are you. The presence of turbulence does not mean you're off course. It may be a sign you're moving into a higher altitude.

STORMS – EXTERNAL OPPOSITION

"When thou passest through the waters, I will be with thee; and through the rivers, they shall not overflow thee: when thou walkest through the fire, thou shalt not be burned; neither shall the flame kindle upon thee." —*Isaiah 43:2*

Storms in flight are visible. Pilots must make quick decisions to fly around, above, or through them. Spiritually, storms represent external trials—attacks from the enemy, sickness, loss, betrayal, or spiritual warfare.

Jesus didn't promise a storm-free life, but He promised His presence in the storm (see Mark 4:35–41). Remember, the storm didn't cancel the disciples' destination—it just became a classroom for faith.

What to do in a storm:

- Stay calm in Christ.
- Listen to His voice, not the wind.
- Hold to the Word—your compass and anchor.

WIND SHEAR – SUDDEN SHIFTS

"Beloved, think it not strange concerning the fiery trial which is to try you, as though some strange thing happened unto you:" **—1 Peter 4:12**

Wind shear is a sudden change in wind speed or direction. It's dangerous in flight because it can destabilize the aircraft. Spiritually, wind shear is when life suddenly shifts—one moment you're soaring, and the next, you're struggling to keep steady.

Sudden shifts might look like:

- Unexpected job loss.
- Ministry disruption.
- Financial crisis.
- Rapid betrayal by someone close.

These moments require immediate spiritual response: prayer, discernment, and staying rooted. Don't panic—adjust. Pilots are trained to recognize and respond. So are you.

Pastor Dr. Claudine Benjamin

INSTRUMENT MALFUNCTION – INTERNAL CONFUSION

"Trust in the Lord with all thine heart; and lean not unto thine own understanding." —**Proverbs 3:5**

What happens when the guidance systems falter? In aviation, instrument malfunction can confuse even the best pilot. Spiritually, this happens when our inner compass feels off—when prayer seems dry, direction unclear, and our emotions cloud discernment.

In these moments, we walk not by sight but by faith.

Trust God even when:

- You don't feel His presence.
- Your plans aren't working.
- The future feels hidden.

Sometimes, God removes the feeling so we develop faith-based flying, not just feeling-based faith.

HOW TO HANDLE DISTURBANCES

STAY IN COMMUNICATION

Pilots never fly blind. They constantly stay in contact with air traffic control. In our spiritual journey, prayer is our lifeline. Constant communion with God keeps us from panic when pressure hits.

"Pray without ceasing." —*1 Thessalonians 5:17*

RELY ON YOUR TRAINING

Pilots are trained in simulators to handle real-world crises. Likewise, your time in the Word, prayer, fasting, and previous storms have trained you for what's ahead. Don't forget what you learned in the calm when you're in the chaos.

TRUST THE DESIGN

Airplanes are built to withstand more than most passengers realize. You are too. You were designed to fly through disturbance, not fall because of it. God's grace and purpose are built into your spiritual frame.

"Ye are of God, little children, and have overcome them: because greater is he that is in you, than he that is in the world." —*1 John 4:4*

THE PURPOSE OF DISTURBANCE

Sometimes, God uses turbulence to wake us up, storms to strengthen us, and unexpected shifts to re-align us with His will. Disturbances challenge us, but they also prepare us.

You learn how to:

- Fly by faith, not sight.
- Stay steady in storms.
- Hear God's voice more clearly.
- Trust God's sovereignty, even when the path seems unclear.

Pastor Dr. Claudine Benjamin

Disturbances in flight are not signs that you're going to crash. They're reminders that you're flying. No turbulence, storm, or shift can bring you down when you are held up by the power of the Holy Spirit, guided by the Word, and covered by the grace of God.

Keep flying. Even if the winds shake you, you were born to rise above it.

"Beloved, think it not strange concerning the fiery trial which is to try you, as though some strange thing happened unto you:" —1 Peter 4:12

Every flight, no matter how well-planned or expertly piloted, encounters disturbances. Whether it's turbulence, wind shear, storms, or system malfunctions, these disruptions are expected parts of flying. They can be uncomfortable—even dangerous—but they are not uncommon.

The same is true in our spiritual lives. When you decide to soar— to rise in purpose, calling, obedience, and growth—you will face disturbances. But these moments don't mean you've taken a wrong turn. They often mean you're on the right path, moving forward and climbing higher.

God doesn't promise a disturbance-free flight, but He does promise presence, purpose, and power through it.

Let's examine the spiritual meaning behind these flight disruptions and how we are equipped to rise through them.

TURBULENCE – THE UNSEEN SHAKE-UP

NATURAL PARALLEL

In aviation, turbulence is caused by unseen shifts in the atmosphere—variations in wind or temperature that disrupt the plane's smooth path. Passengers often feel uneasy when turbulence hits, even if the aircraft is still safely under control.

SPIRITUAL LESSON

Spiritual turbulence is what you feel when you're doing everything right—but still feel shaken. You're praying, fasting, serving, and giving—but suddenly, your peace is disturbed. You may not see the source, but the effect is real.

Examples of Spiritual Turbulence:

- Internal restlessness or emotional overwhelm.
- Delay in answers to prayer.
- Resistance from unexpected places.
- Confusion about your next steps.

BIBLICAL INSIGHT

Paul experienced turbulence during ministry: *"For a great door and effectual is opened unto me, and there are many adversaries."* **—1 Corinthians 16:9**

Even open doors can come with shaking.

Your Response: Stay buckled in your faith. Don't jump out of purpose because of temporary discomfort. Turbulence is often a sign that you're moving forward and breaking into a new spiritual layer.

STORMS – THE EXTERNAL BATTLES

NATURAL PARALLEL

Storms are visible, dramatic, and sometimes violent. They can disrupt communication, reduce visibility, and require rerouting. Pilots either fly around them, over them, or through them with precision and calm.

SPIRITUAL LESSON

Storms represent external opposition—attacks from the enemy, personal crises, loss, betrayal, or spiritual warfare. They threaten to cloud your vision and make you feel disconnected from God.

Examples of Spiritual Storms:

- Financial collapse or loss of provision.
- Sudden illness or death of a loved one.
- Intense betrayal in ministry or personal relationships.
- Severe spiritual attacks during seasons of growth.

BIBLICAL INSIGHT

Jesus calmed the storm in Mark 4:35–41. But before He did, He slept through it—teaching us that peace is not the absence of storms but the presence of trust.

In Full Flight

Your Response: Anchor yourself in the Word and refuse to panic. Command peace into your soul. Speak to the storm in faith. Not every storm is from the devil—some are training grounds for greater trust and power.

WIND SHEAR – SUDDEN SHIFTS

NATURAL PARALLEL

Wind shear is a sudden change in wind direction or speed that causes instability, especially during takeoff or landing. It's dangerous because it can cause unexpected dips or shifts in altitude.

SPIRITUAL LESSON

Wind shear mirrors the sudden shifts we experience in life—things we didn't see coming. It could be a spiritual promotion you weren't ready for or a demotion that caught you off guard. Either way, it causes a moment of instability.

Examples of Spiritual Wind Shear:

- A door suddenly opens or closes.
- A major relationship ends or begins.
- Unexpected relocation or transition.
- A prophetic word shifts your direction.

BIBLICAL INSIGHT

Joseph experienced this when he went from prisoner to palace in one day (see Genesis 41). That kind of elevation brings its own turbulence.

139

Pastor Dr. Claudine Benjamin

Your Response: Quickly align with God's voice. Sudden shifts demand immediate spiritual flexibility. Stay grounded in your identity so the shift doesn't shake your confidence in God's plan.

INSTRUMENT MALFUNCTION – WHEN VISION FEELS OFF

NATURAL PARALLEL

If an aircraft's instruments fail, it becomes difficult to navigate. Pilots rely heavily on internal systems for guidance—especially in darkness or poor weather. Malfunction can result in wrong altitude, misdirection, or loss of communication.

SPIRITUAL LESSON

There are times in our walk when our internal systems—our emotions, sense of direction, or spiritual discernment—feel off. We don't feel God the way we used to. Prayer feels dry. Worship feels heavy. Our spiritual senses seem disconnected.

Examples of Instrument Malfunction:

- Spiritual dryness
- Burnout
- Loss of motivation or joy
- Confusion about purpose

BIBLICAL INSIGHT

David cried out, *"Why art thou cast down, O my soul? and why art thou disquieted in me? hope thou in God: for I shall yet praise him for the help of his countenance."* —**Psalm 42:5**. Even spiritual giants feel lost sometimes.

Your Response: Trust God's last instruction until He gives a new one. Don't make rash decisions during disconnection. Remember: feelings are not facts. Fly by the Word, not by emotion.

BIRD STRIKES – UNEXPECTED ATTACKS

NATURAL PARALLEL

Bird strikes are sudden collisions between planes and birds, often during takeoff or landing. Though small, they can damage engines or cause emergency landings.

SPIRITUAL LESSON

Not all disturbances are grand or visible—some come as small distractions, critics, or offenses that hit at just the wrong time. These "bird strikes" are designed to sabotage your momentum.

BIBLICAL INSIGHT

Nehemiah faced constant "bird strikes" in the form of ridicule and distractions: *"And conspired all of them together to come and to fight against Jerusalem, and to hinder it."* —**Nehemiah 4:8**

Your Response: Protect your atmosphere. Guard your mind and spirit. Don't let small things knock you out of position. Keep flying.

HOW TO RESPOND TO DISTURBANCES

1. Stay Connected to the Control Tower

Maintain open communication with heaven through prayer, worship, and the Word.

2. Stay Buckled in Faith

Don't get up in panic. Trust that the One who called you to fly has built you to withstand the journey.

3. Rely on the Flight Manual

The Bible is your guide. Review God's promises. They were written to help you navigate.

4. Know That You Are Not Alone

Pilots fly with co-pilots and air traffic controllers. Spiritually, you're not flying solo. The Holy Spirit is your constant guide.

FINAL DESCENT: DON'T ABORT THE MISSION

When turbulence hits, some consider giving up. Don't. Disturbance is not a sign to abort the mission—it's a sign that you're moving. Stay the course. There's breakthrough above the clouds.

In Full Flight

Remember, you are not built to crash. You are built to soar—through disturbances, over storms, and into divine destiny.

REFLECTION QUESTIONS

1. What type of spiritual disturbance are you currently experiencing?

2. How have you responded in past seasons of turbulence?

3. What specific scriptures can you cling to during this current flight season?

PRAYER

Lord, help me stay steady through the shaking. Strengthen my faith during turbulence, sharpen my focus in storms, and stabilize my emotions in spiritual wind shear. Remind me that Your Spirit guides every flight and that I'm not alone in the sky. In Jesus' name. Amen.

CHAPTER 17

COPING WITH DISTURBANCES IN FULL FLIGHT – SPIRITUALLY AND PHYSICALLY

"He giveth power to the faint; and to them that have no might he increaseth strength. Even the youths shall faint and be weary, and the young men shall utterly fall: But they that wait upon the Lord shall renew their strength; they shall mount up with wings as eagles; they shall run, and not be weary; and they shall walk, and not faint." —Isaiah 40:29–31

Reaching full flight—whether in the natural or spiritual— requires effort, coordination, and strength. But maintaining that flight through disturbances requires something deeper: resilience, awareness, and trust.

Disturbances don't just try to stop our ascent; they aim to disrupt our stability once we are already in motion. Whether in the cockpit of a plane or the center of a spiritual assignment, how we cope in the middle of the journey determines whether we finish strong or fall short.

145

Pastor Dr. Claudine Benjamin

UNDERSTANDING DISTURBANCES: THE REALITY OF RESISTANCE

In both aviation and our Christian journey, disturbances are inevitable. No aircraft climbs to cruising altitude without hitting some kind of resistance. No believer walks in purpose without trials, spiritual turbulence, or opposition.

Disturbances may not be signs of danger—they're often signs of momentum.

COPING WITH PHYSICAL DISTURBANCES IN FLIGHT

1. Turbulence and Passenger Anxiety

Physical Reality: Turbulence often causes fear in passengers— even though it's rarely dangerous. It's the discomfort of the unknown, the shaking, and the loss of control that causes panic.

Coping Mechanism:

- **Trust the pilot:** Remind yourself that the crew is trained for this.

- **Stay calm:** Panic doesn't change the turbulence; peace helps you endure it.

- **Adjust posture:** Sit back, fasten your seatbelt, breathe, and ride it out.

In Full Flight

Spiritual Parallel: When life shakes you, the key is to trust the One flying the plane—Jesus. He's not shaken by your turbulence.

2. Storms and Re-Routing

Physical Reality: Storms may require the plane to reroute, delay landing, or alter altitude. It's not a failure—it's wisdom.

Coping Mechanism:

- **Stay flexible:** Trust that rerouting is protection, not punishment.

- **Accept delays:** Delay does not mean denial.

- **Follow instructions:** Listen for announcements and guidance from the crew.

Spiritual Parallel: God will sometimes change your path to protect you from what you can't see. What feels like a setback is often strategic redirection.

3. Altitude Sickness and Physical Discomfort

Physical Reality: High altitudes can cause discomfort, like ear pressure, fatigue, or dizziness. The body needs time to adjust to new levels.

Coping Mechanism:

- Stay hydrated.

Pastor Dr. Claudine Benjamin

- Adjust slowly.

- Use tools (earplugs, meds, breathing techniques).

Spiritual Parallel: Spiritually, higher altitudes can bring loneliness, new pressure, and unfamiliar responsibility. Growth requires adjustment. The higher you go, the thinner the air—but the clearer the vision.

COPING WITH SPIRITUAL DISTURBANCES IN

FLIGHT

1. When Prayer Feels Dry

Even as you soar in purpose, there will be moments when your prayer life feels mechanical or distant.

How to Cope:

- **Shift your environment:** Find a new worship space or prayer walk.
- **Pray the Word:** When you can't find your words, use His.
- **Be honest:** God honors real prayers over rehearsed ones.

2. When Spiritual Warfare Increases

Elevation invites opposition. The higher you fly, the more visible you become to the enemy. Disturbances may intensify as you approach new levels of breakthrough.

In Full Flight

How to Cope:

- Increase your discernment.
- Stay armored (see Ephesians 6:10–18).
- Partner with intercessors. Don't fly solo in warfare.

3. When You Feel Like Quitting Mid-Flight

There will be times you want to give up—on the ministry, on the dream, even on the journey. The flight gets long, the resistance grows fierce, and the destination feels far.

How to Cope:

- Look back at your why.
- Take spiritual rest—but don't abort the mission.
- Speak to your soul like David did (see Psalm 42:5).

SPIRITUAL SELF-TALK

"I've come too far to quit now. I may be tired, but I'm still flying. I may be shaken, but I'm still airborne. God brought me this far, and He will carry me the rest of the way."

STAY THE COURSE

You were never promised a flight without disturbance—but you were promised God's presence in every phase. The pilot of your soul is not surprised by turbulence, storms, or pressure. He's trained, sovereign, and in control.

149

Pastor Dr. Claudine Benjamin

Let this be your declaration in full flight:

"Though the winds shake me, they will not break me.
Though the clouds hide my view, my God sees it all.
Though the storms roar, my spirit will rest.
I was born to fly—and I will finish this flight in victory."

REFLECTION QUESTIONS

1. What physical or emotional disturbances have tested your stability lately?

2. How do you typically respond when spiritual turbulence hits?

3. What practical tools can help you manage both your physical health and spiritual wellness in flight?

PHYSICAL DISTURBANCES IN FLIGHT AND HOW THEY MIRROR LIFE

1. Turbulence – Discomfort Without Danger

In Flight: Turbulence causes sudden shaking, usually due to air pressure changes or jet streams. It's rarely dangerous but always uncomfortable. It reminds passengers that although they're in the air, they are not in control.

In Life: Turbulence happens when we feel the discomfort of change or resistance. You may be progressing in life, but a job shifts, relationships are tested, or you're hit with stress you didn't expect. Everything feels unsteady—even though you're still secure in God.

How to Cope:

- **Remain seated in peace:** Don't move when God hasn't told you to.
- **Buckle in the Word:** Meditate on Scriptures like Psalm 46:1–3 and John 14:27.
- **Trust the process:** Turbulence is a sign that you are in motion, not that you're in trouble.

2. Storms – External Forces That Interrupt Your Flow

In Flight: Storms force pilots to change course. Heavy rain, lightning, or wind conditions can block visibility and threaten control, so they must fly above or around the system.

In Life: Storms show up as sickness, betrayal, financial trouble, grief, or family conflict. You were flying fine, and now a storm is threatening to bring you down.

Biblical Example: In Mark 4:35–41, Jesus and His disciples faced a literal storm. While the storm raged, Jesus slept. When the disciples panicked, He woke up and calmed the storm with a word.

How to Cope:

- **Speak the Word:** Declare peace. Speak authority over your situation.

151

Pastor Dr. Claudine Benjamin

- **Don't jump ship:** Stay in the boat. Stay with Jesus.

- **Shift altitude if needed:** Sometimes, the storm forces you into a new level of prayer or dependence.

3. Wind Shear – Sudden Shifts That Change Everything

In Flight: Wind shear causes rapid changes in wind direction or speed. It's dangerous because it affects altitude and balance. Planes must respond immediately to avoid losing control.

In Life: This is when life shifts without warning—a promotion, a loss, a major decision, a new door opening, or an old one slamming shut. It disorients you spiritually and emotionally.

Biblical Example: Joseph experienced wind shear when he went from prison to palace in one day (see Genesis 41). Sudden shifts can elevate you or humble you—but God uses both.

How to Cope:

- **Anchor in prayer:** Don't rush decisions in transition.
- **Recalibrate your heart:** God's sudden shifts are still under His sovereignty.
- **Submit to new direction:** Every shift is a setup for His glory.

4. Altitude Pressure – Discomfort in Higher Places

In Flight: The higher a plane flies, the thinner the air. Passengers may experience headaches, pressure, or fatigue. The body must adjust to the new level.

In Life: New spiritual heights bring new demands. You prayed for elevation—but now you're tired, isolated, misunderstood, and stretched.

Biblical Example: Elijah, after calling down fire from heaven, experienced pressure so intense he wanted to die (see 1 Kings 19). Elevation comes with exposure.

How to Cope:

- **Practice spiritual rest:** Find time to recharge in God's presence.
- **Stay hydrated in the Spirit:** Drink deeply of the Word and worship.
- **Don't misinterpret pressure as punishment:** It's part of the process of growth.

SPIRITUAL DISTURBANCES AND YOUR INNER RESPONSE

1. When God Feels Silent

You've taken flight, but now you can't hear His voice. You're doing everything right—praying, fasting, obeying—but it feels like heaven is closed.

How to Cope:

- **Fly by the last instruction:** Don't land just because you haven't received a new word.

153

Pastor Dr. Claudine Benjamin

- **Keep worshipping:** Silence doesn't mean absence.
- **Review His promises:** Remember what He already said.

2. When Warfare Intensifies

Elevation attracts attention. The enemy won't fight you over where you've been—he fights you for where you're going. Resistance increases at higher levels.

Biblical Example: Daniel fasted for 21 days, and his answer was delayed due to spiritual warfare in the heavens (see Daniel 10:12–13).

How to Cope:

- Put on spiritual armor (see Ephesians 6:10–18).
- Pray with authority—not fear.
- Partner with intercessors. No pilot flies alone; neither should you.

3. When You're Tempted to Quit

The flight is long. The fatigue is real. The destination feels distant. You're tempted to go back to what's comfortable and familiar.

How to Cope:

- **Declare God's faithfulness:** *"I had fainted, unless I had believed to see the goodness of the Lord in the land of the living." —Psalm 27:13*
- **Refuse to land early:** Just because you're tired doesn't mean it's time to stop.

In Full Flight

- **Ask for fresh wind:** The Holy Spirit renews your strength.

COPING TOOLS: YOUR SPIRITUAL FLIGHT KIT

1. **The Word (Your Manual):** Keep the Word open and in your mouth (see Joshua 1:8).

2. **Prayer (Your Communication Line):** Keep talking to the Control Tower.

3. **Fellowship (Your Co-Pilot Network):** Stay connected to those who can lift you when you're weak.

4. **Rest (Your Recovery Tool):** Don't glorify burnout—take Sabbath moments.

5. **Worship (Your Altitude Adjuster):** Worship shifts focus from the storm to the Savior.

YOU ARE CLEARED FOR A SAFE LANDING

Disturbances may come—but they won't destroy you. You're not flying blind. Your Pilot is in control. He knows the destination, the altitude, the route, and the ETA.

God is not just with you on the runway—He's with you in the air. He knows how to guide you through storms, empower you in turbulence, and land you safely in His purpose.

REFLECTION QUESTIONS

1. What kind of disturbance are you currently facing—turbulence, a storm, a sudden shift?

2. How have you responded to past flight disturbances in your spiritual walk?

3. What truths from God's Word can you apply when flying through difficulty?

PRAYER

God, when turbulence shakes my journey, help me to remain steady in You. Teach me to respond and not react, to rest and not fear. Strengthen my spiritual instincts and help me remember that You are always in control, even when the path is bumpy.

Scripture: Philippians 4:6-7 – *"Be careful for nothing; but in every thing by prayer and supplication with thanksgiving let your requests be made known unto God. And the peace of God, which passeth all understanding, shall keep your hearts and minds through Christ Jesus."*

CHAPTER 18

THE DANGERS OF MID-FLIGHT DRIFT

STAYING FOCUSED AT HIGH ALTITUDE – THE RISK OF SPIRITUAL STALL

You're in the air. You've broken past fear, pushed through resistance, and finally gained the momentum to soar. But something subtle begins to creep in—not a crash, not a storm, not even fatigue. It's *drift*. Slow. Undetectable. Dangerous. It's the silent sabotage of staying aloft without staying aligned.

In aviation, a mid-flight drift occurs when a pilot loses course without immediate realization. The aircraft continues to fly, but it's no longer headed in the right direction. In the spirit, the same principle applies—when we lose focus, lose fire, or lose intentionality, we may still be "active" but not advancing in purpose.

THE SUBTLETY OF DRIFT

Drift rarely feels dramatic. It starts with skipping a prayer, neglecting the Word, tuning out from accountability, or growing numb to conviction. Unlike turbulence, it doesn't jolt you—it lulls you.

Pastor Dr. Claudine Benjamin

That's what makes it so dangerous.

Just as a pilot must frequently check instruments to ensure the plane stays on course, believers must constantly assess spiritual bearings. What you're ignoring now can cost you later.

Drift Symptoms:

- Decreased passion for purpose.
- Increased distractions.
- Numbness to spiritual things.
- Routine replacing relationship with God.
- Gradual compromise of convictions.

Flight Lesson: Drift is rarely due to direction change—it's due to attention loss.

STAYING FOCUSED AT HIGH ALTITUDE

Reaching a high altitude in the spirit—clarity, peace, purpose—requires more than elevation; it demands focus. High altitudes require sharper vision and steadier hands. The higher you go, the more susceptible you are to distractions dressed as opportunities or spiritual pride masked as strength.

Eli, the young eagle, discovers that it's easier to soar than it is to stay focused mid-flight. He begins looking around instead of ahead. Zara, the seasoned soarer, gently reminds him: *"The higher you fly, the more focused you must become. Not every wind is your wind."*

158

In Full Flight

To stay focused:

- Stay anchored in God's voice (see John 10:27).
- Remain teachable and accountable.
- Keep your eyes on the mission, not just the motion.
- Celebrate wins, but don't settle in them.

Flight Reminder: Altitude doesn't make you invincible—it makes you responsible.

THE RISK OF SPIRITUAL STALL

Stalling in aviation happens when the aircraft's lift is insufficient to sustain flight. In spiritual terms, stalling occurs when our faith is not fueled by fresh intimacy with God. You can't live off yesterday's revelation. What lifted you last season won't always sustain you in this one.

Stall often happens in the lives of:

- Leaders running on empty.
- Believers doing ministry without devotion.
- Dreamers who stopped praying but kept planning.
- Passionate people who neglected rest and renewal.

You don't always fall from flight because of sin. Sometimes you stall from burnout. That's why rest, focus, and connection to God are essential at every altitude.

Flight Warning: If the engine of your spirit is sputtering, don't fake the flight—refuel.

159

COURSE CORRECTION IS POSSIBLE

The beauty of flying with the Holy Spirit as your pilot is that mid-flight corrections are not only possible—they're expected. Grace makes it possible to get back on course, but truth requires we admit we've drifted.

To correct your flight path:

1. Acknowledge where you've veered.
2. Recalibrate your purpose with prayer and the Word.
3. Seek accountability from a trusted source.
4. Reignite your passion through worship and solitude.
5. Recommit to the mission—not just the movement.

Even the most seasoned eagles need realignment. Obed, the weathered eagle, shares that some of his greatest lessons came from correcting his course in mid-flight. *"It's not weakness to adjust—it's wisdom,"* he says. *"The goal isn't just to stay up—it's to finish well."*

FLY WITH FOCUS, FINISH WITH FIRE

Mid-flight drift doesn't mean it's over—it means it's time to refocus. It's a divine warning that you can't afford to fly on autopilot. The enemy doesn't have to crash you—he just wants you off course. But you were created to fly on purpose, with purpose, for purpose.

Stay alert. Stay aligned. And soar.

In Full Flight

PRAYER

Father, protect me from spiritual drift. Help me to stay on course and not lose sight of my mission. Keep my heart from complacency and my spirit from distraction. Let my focus be sharpened by Your Word and my direction anchored in Your truth.

Scripture: Hebrews 2:1 – *"Therefore we ought to give the more earnest heed to the things which we have heard, lest at any time we should let them slip."*

CHAPTER 19

MIDAIR MAINTENANCE

PRAYER, FASTING, AND SPIRITUAL TUNE-UPS – BUILDING ALTITUDE AWARENESS

As every seasoned pilot knows, staying airborne isn't just about takeoff—it's about maintenance in motion. Midair maintenance is the act of assessing, adjusting, and attending to your spiritual condition while you're already in flight. It's what keeps you soaring when others are stalling. In the realm of spiritual flight, our "engine checks" come through consistent prayer, intentional fasting, and periodic spiritual tune-ups. These practices aren't optional—they're essential.

THE POWER OF PRAYER: THE OXYGEN OF THE SOARING LIFE

Prayer is not merely a lifeline; it is the very oxygen of a purpose-driven life. It connects you to divine instruction, fuels your discernment, and keeps your spiritual engines aligned with the will of God. Without prayer, altitude becomes unsustainable. You may find yourself gliding without power, slowly descending into distraction, discouragement, or defeat.

163

Jesus demonstrated this throughout His ministry. Even amid miracles and movement, He withdrew often to pray. He taught His disciples to do the same, showing us that prayer inflight sustains direction and discernment.

Midair Insight: When you stop praying, you start drifting. The voice of the Father grows faint. The turbulence of life grows louder. Prayer silences the noise and recalibrates your compass.

THE FIRE OF FASTING: BURN AWAY THE WEIGHT

While prayer aligns your spirit, fasting purifies it. Fasting is the act of surrendering natural sustenance to receive supernatural strength. It's how you burn off unnecessary weight in your spiritual cabin—the bitterness, fear, complacency, or confusion that slows you down.

Fasting clears the spiritual atmosphere. It humbles your flesh so your spirit can soar. It increases your sensitivity to the Holy Spirit and tunes your ears to divine frequency.

When Jesus was led into the wilderness, He fasted. Before His greatest public display of power came a private sacrifice. The wilderness wasn't a pause; it was preparation. So it is with us. Fasting isn't punishment—it's purification.

Midair Insight: Altitude and attitude are linked. Fasting helps adjust both.

SPIRITUAL TUNE-UPS: MAINTENANCE PREVENTS MAYDAY

Even a soaring eagle must occasionally adjust its wings, check its feathers, and assess its bearings. Likewise, spiritual maintenance prevents a mayday situation—a cry for help when things spiral out of control.

These tune-ups may come through:

- Personal retreats.
- Consistent time in the Word.
- Accountability from spiritual mentors.
- Worship that revives the soul.
- Journaling your spiritual progress.

Maintenance isn't just about fixing what's broken—it's about preventing breakdowns before they begin.

Midair Insight: Don't wait for a crisis to check your spiritual condition. Tune up while things are going well so you're ready when they're not.

BUILDING ALTITUDE AWARENESS: KNOWING WHEN YOU'RE DRIFTING

One of the enemy's tactics is gradual descent. He won't always push you into a nosedive—he'll just subtly pull you out of your assigned altitude. Altitude awareness means being honest about where you are spiritually, emotionally, and mentally.

Pastor Dr. Claudine Benjamin

Are you:

- Coasting when you should be climbing?
- Straining when you should be soaring?
- Isolated when you should be accountable?

Ask the Holy Spirit to help you check your internal altimeter. Learn to recognize the signs that you're drifting, fatigued, or overburdened. It's not weakness to notice—it's wisdom.

KEEP SOARING BY STAYING ALIGNED

Midair maintenance is what keeps purpose alive. The young eagle, Eli, must learn this, the soaring eagle, Zara, lives by this, and the weathered eagle, Obed, teaches it with wisdom. They all know that soaring is a result of discipline, not just desire.

Stay prayerful. Stay sensitive. Stay maintained. And watch God take you even higher.

PRAYER

Lord, I acknowledge my need for constant maintenance while I soar. Examine my heart, renew my mind, and strengthen my spirit. Repair any areas that have become worn, and remove anything that could hinder my flight. Keep me sensitive to Your promptings and submitted to Your care.

Scripture: Psalm 51:10 – *"Create in me a clean heart, O God; and renew a right spirit within me."*

CHAPTER 20

KNOWING WHEN TO DESCEND

DIVINE ASSIGNMENTS IN LOWER ALTITUDES –
SERVING WITHOUT LOSING HEIGHT

"But it shall not be so among you: but whosoever will be great among you, let him be your minister; And whosoever will be chief among you, let him be your servant: Even as the Son of man came not to be ministered unto, but to minister, and to give his life a ransom for many." —**Matthew 20:26–28**

Soaring is beautiful. Reaching high places, attaining spiritual altitude, seeing with clarity, and experiencing freedom in Christ are all part of the promise of walking in divine purpose. But full flight is not just about staying up—it's about knowing **when to descend**, how to serve from your elevation, and how to carry out God's assignments without compromising your calling.

Every great pilot knows that **landing is just as important as flying.** Descending is not always a sign of failure—it's often a sign of **mission.** There are times when God calls the soaring soul to return to lower altitudes—not to fall, but to fulfill.

167

Pastor Dr. Claudine Benjamin

This chapter is about embracing the wisdom of knowing **when to come down**, how to serve on the ground while maintaining heavenly altitude, and how to carry out divine assignments in humility, purpose, and power.

THE DESCENT IS STRATEGIC, NOT SHAMEFUL

There's a misconception in spiritual circles that descending—or stepping away from a spotlight, pausing a platform, or shifting into a servant role—is equivalent to losing your "anointing" or status. Nothing could be further from the truth.

Even **Jesus descended**.

"But made himself of no reputation, and took upon him the form of a servant, and was made in the likeness of men:" —Philippians 2:7

The King of kings **left the heights of heaven** to dwell among us. He **descended** into humanity, into suffering, into service, not because He was weak—but because He was **mission-minded**.

There will be times in your life when you will hear the voice of the Holy Spirit prompting you to descend—to enter a season of **hiddenness, humility, or help**. This is not a demotion. It is **divine positioning.**

Sometimes, your greatest impact is not made from the sky—but from the ground.

168

DIVINE ASSIGNMENTS IN LOWER ALTITUDES

As believers, our altitude is spiritual. But our **assignment is often earthly**. We are seated in heavenly places (see Ephesians 2:6) but called to walk in real places—with real people, real pain, and real problems.

God may ask you to:

- Step down from leading to mentor others.
- Leave a high-visibility position to care for your family.
- Pause your pursuit of influence to pour into someone broken.
- Walk alongside someone who's grounded, helping them rise again.

This is not the abandonment of calling—this is the **embodiment of Christ.**

Jesus descended into towns, villages, leper colonies, homes, and gardens. He washed feet, touched the sick, and ate with sinners. And not once did He lose His authority by coming low.

Your calling is not compromised when you descend—it's confirmed.

KNOWING THE DIFFERENCE: FALLING VERSUS DESCENDING

It's important to discern whether you're descending by obedience or falling from distraction or disobedience.

Pastor Dr. Claudine Benjamin

Falling happens when:

- You disconnect from God's voice.
- You compromise your convictions.
- You grow careless with character.
- You prioritize performance over intimacy.

Descending happens when:

- God calls you to serve someone who can't reach your current level.
- You pause to heal or restore others.
- You teach, train, and build without needing a title.
- You return to a place where God has assigned you to bring elevation.

One is prideful collapse. The other is purposeful obedience.

Ask yourself:

- "Am I flying in alignment with God's voice?"
- "Is this a descent or a decline?"
- "Is this sacrifice or sabotage?"

There is wisdom in intentional descent—and danger in unnoticed drift.

SERVING WITHOUT LOSING HEIGHT

Here's the beauty of divine flight: You can serve from the ground while staying connected to the skies.

170

In the natural, when a plane descends, it doesn't stop being a plane. It simply adjusts its altitude based on the mission. Likewise, when you serve in lower places, your identity, value, and calling remain unchanged.

Jesus washed His disciples' feet—and was still the Savior of the world.

How to serve without losing spiritual altitude:

- **Stay rooted in prayer.** Let your intimacy with God remain high.
- **Stay full of the Word.** Don't let busyness rob you of daily bread.
- **Stay submitted.** Even in serving, you are still under orders from the Pilot.
- **Stay sensitive.** Don't miss your next launch while serving on the ground.

You are not meant to live in burnout, exhaustion, or performance. Serving from a full place allows you to remain elevated, even while moving through "lower" roles.

WHEN SERVING LOOKS LIKE SURRENDER

There are seasons when God may ask you to let go of a dream, pause a project, or take a backseat to someone else's breakthrough. These are not moments of abandonment—they are invitations into deeper trust.

Surrendering a stage doesn't mean surrendering your calling.

Pastor Dr. Claudine Benjamin

Laying something down doesn't mean God has forgotten what He placed in you.

Sometimes God asks you to descend so He can **refine your heart, reset your focus, or realign your assignment.** And when you descend in surrender, He always raises you again in strength.
"Humble yourselves therefore under the mighty hand of God, that he may exalt you in due time:" —*1 Peter 5:6*

THE BLESSING OF THE GROUND

Lower altitudes teach you:

- Compassion
- Patience
- Perspective
- The value of people
- The importance of preparation

You'll find **blessing in the descent** if you look for it.

Ask the nurse caring for patients, the teacher shaping young minds, the single mother pouring into her children, the counselor guiding broken souls, the pastor planting seeds in silence—they've touched more lives from the "ground" than many ever will from platforms.

You don't have to fly to be effective. Sometimes, your most fruitful season will be in the fields.

In Full Flight

KNOWING WHEN TO RISE AGAIN

Every descent has a purpose—but it's not permanent. There will come a time when the Holy Spirit whispers, *"It's time to climb again."*

Recognize when:

- The assignment is complete.
- The lesson has been learned.
- The anointing is shifting.
- The fire is returning.

Don't grow so comfortable on the ground that you forget how to soar. And don't grow so proud in flight that you resist the descent.

Obedience must rule both seasons.

DESCENT IS PART OF THE FLIGHT PLAN

No aircraft stays in the air forever. **Every flight has a descent strategy.** Not to crash—but to land with precision and purpose. And often, the next takeoff requires a good landing first.

If you find yourself in a season where God has brought you low— *know this:* You're not forgotten. You're not broken. You're not beneath anyone. You are **exactly where He needs you to be**.

Whether flying high or serving low, **you are still in flight.** You are still in purpose. God is still piloting your journey.

173

Pastor Dr. Claudine Benjamin

REFLECTION QUESTIONS

1. Are you in a season of descent or elevation?
2. Have you equated descending with failure, rather than service?
3. How can you remain spiritually elevated while serving in earthly assignments?
4. What lessons is God teaching you in this season on the ground?

PRAYER

Heavenly Father, give me discernment to know when it is time to descend. Help me not to resist Your leading when You're guiding me to rest, serve, or prepare for a new season. Teach me that even in descending, I am still walking in purpose and obedience.

Scripture: Ecclesiastes 3:1 – *"To every thing there is a season, and a time to every purpose under the heaven:"*

CHAPTER 21

PURPOSE UNFOLDED IN MOTION

WALKING OUT DESTINY WHILE STILL SOARING –

THE IMPACT OF A LIFE LIVED IN FULL FLIGHT

"Being confident of this very thing, that he which hath begun a good work in you will perform it until the day of Jesus Christ:" — **Philippians 1:6**

Purpose is not a place we arrive at. It is a path we walk. It's not a destination—it's a **living, breathing, unfolding journey**, crafted by the hand of God and made clearer with each obedient step.

Many believe that purpose is revealed in a single moment—a lightning strike of clarity that tells you who you are and what you're meant to do. But in reality, **purpose unfolds in motion.** It's revealed not in stillness alone but in flight. As you obey, as you trust, as you soar—even through stormy skies—your destiny becomes visible.

This chapter is an invitation to keep flying **even when the details aren't finished,** to keep showing up even when you don't feel

Pastor Dr. Claudine Benjamin

"ready," and to believe that the impact of your life is already happening—even while you're still becoming.

YOU DON'T NEED TO HAVE IT ALL FIGURED OUT

TO BE IN PURPOSE

God rarely gives the full blueprint up front. Like Abram, who was told to *"Go to a land I will show you"* (see Genesis 12:1), we are often given just enough light for the next step. The temptation is to pause, to wait for all the answers before launching into the next level. But faith moves first. And **motion invites revelation.**

Your calling doesn't require perfection. It requires **movement**.

Even when you feel unqualified, insecure, or unfinished, God can still use you:

- **Moses had a speech problem**—God used him to deliver a nation.
- **David was a shepherd boy**—God used him to slay giants and become king.
- **Esther was an orphan**—God used her to preserve a people.

You may feel like you're "in process," but heaven sees you as purposeful.

Your wings don't have to be polished. Your path doesn't have to be smooth. Purpose begins when you say yes—even if it's messy, imperfect, and unclear.

176

DESTINY IS NOT A MOMENT—IT'S A LIFESTYLE

We sometimes think we're "on purpose" only when we're on a stage, behind a pulpit, leading a business, or achieving a milestone. But **purpose is not a title—it's obedience.** It's being faithful to God's instruction, no matter how big or small.

Jesus didn't just fulfill His purpose on the cross—He lived it every single day. He was walking in destiny when He healed the sick, when He withdrew to pray, when He spoke to the woman at the well, and when He wept with Mary and Martha.

Likewise, your **daily obedience**, hidden faithfulness, consistent growth—all of it is shaping the impact of your life. You don't "arrive" at purpose. You **walk it out in motion**—step by step, wingbeat by wingbeat.

YOUR FLIGHT INSPIRES OTHERS

You may not realize it, but **people are watching you fly.** Your motion awakens others. When you soar despite past pain, you give others permission to heal. When you pursue God despite loss, you encourage others to trust. When you rise again after crashing, you remind others that failure is not final.

You don't have to be famous to be impactful. Purposeful flight often happens **in secret skies**. Your children, coworkers, church family, community—they are influenced not just by your words but by your **willingness to fly when it's hard.**

Your story, scars, testimony—these are **beacons of hope**. Every mile you fly in purpose becomes **a path cleared for someone else.**

IMPACT IS MEASURED BY OBEDIENCE, NOT APPLAUSE

Sometimes you will be tempted to measure your success by numbers, recognition, or results. But heaven measures by **obedience**.

In Matthew 25, Jesus honored the servants not for how much they gained but for how faithful they were with what they were given. The one who had five talents and gained five more received the same affirmation as the one who had two.

"Well done, good and faithful servant." That's the reward of a life lived in full flight—**not applause, but alignment. Not fame, but faithfulness.**

God doesn't ask you to control the outcome. He asks you to keep flying.

EVEN WHILE SOARING, YOU'RE STILL BECOMING

Some believe that once you step into purpose, you will never struggle again. But flight doesn't eliminate difficulty—it deepens dependence.

Even in full flight, you'll:

- Still face storms.

In Full Flight

- Still need recalibration.
- Still grow in wisdom.
- Still wrestle with flesh.
- Still learn how to land safely, rest, and rise again.

Purpose doesn't mean you are perfect. It means you're surrendered, consistent, and willing. You're **learning in motion**, becoming while building, healing while helping, rising while resting. And that's the beauty of grace: God doesn't wait for you to "arrive" to use you. He uses you in motion.

WALKING AND SOARING: THE BALANCE OF ELEVATION AND EARTH

So how do you live in full flight and still walk out your destiny on the ground? It comes down to **balance**. Purpose requires **both heavenly perspective and earthly obedience.** Like an eagle that flies high but lands to feed, serve, and tend to its young, you must know when to soar in vision and when to walk in discipline.

Jesus moved between mountaintop prayer and village miracles. He lived with heaven in His view but people in His heart.

Your full flight includes:

- Soaring in revelation.
- Landing in service.
- Lifting others while you climb.
- Remaining grounded in humility.
- Trusting the Pilot in all things.

179

Pastor Dr. Claudine Benjamin

Purpose is not just how high you fly—it's how faithfully you walk when your feet touch the ground.

THE LEGACY OF A LIFE IN FULL FLIGHT

When your life is lived in motion, in purpose, and in faith—**you leave a trail**—not just for others to follow but as a testimony to God's goodness, grace, and power.

A life lived in full flight says:

- "I trusted God when I couldn't trace Him."
- "I obeyed even when it hurt."
- "I soared even when I was scared."
- "I crashed, but I didn't quit."
- "I flew with purpose, and I finished my race."

Your legacy is built in the skies you've crossed, the battles you've overcome, and the people you've lifted along the way.

PURPOSE IS STILL UNFOLDING

You are not done. Your story is not over. The skies ahead are still open. And God's plan is still unfolding **in motion**.

Keep flying. Keep walking. Keep trusting.

Your impact is not coming—it's **happening now**.
You are living in purpose.
You are walking in destiny.
You are already **in full flight.**

REFLECTION QUESTIONS

1. In what ways have you delayed movement because you were waiting to feel "ready?"
2. Who has been inspired by watching you soar—even when you didn't feel strong?
3. Are you living daily with purpose, or only waiting for a future "moment"?
4. What steps can you take today to walk out your destiny in motion?

PRAYER:

Lord, I thank You that as I move in obedience, You unfold my purpose. Help me not to wait for every detail but to trust You step by step. As I move forward, reveal more of who You are and what You've designed me to be. I trust You with the process.

Scripture: Psalm 37:23 – *"The steps of a good man are ordered by the Lord: and he delighteth in his way."*

CHAPTER 22

INSPIRING OTHERS TO TAKE THE FLIGHT

BECOMING A CATALYST FOR PURPOSE IN OTHERS

It's one thing to fly—it's another to ignite the skies with others beside you. True soaring isn't selfish. Once you've discovered the joy of spiritual flight, there's a divine responsibility to help others take off. To live inspired is powerful; to inspire others is transformational.

In every eagle's journey, there comes a moment where flight becomes more than personal progress—it becomes purpose for someone else's launch. Whether you are an Eli in discovery, a Zara in rhythm, or an Obed in wisdom, your flight was never meant to be a solo journey. The skies were made for many wings.

THE POWER OF VISIBILITY: YOUR FLIGHT IS A MESSAGE

Your soaring life speaks louder than sermons. When people see you rise despite storms, it gives them permission to believe they can rise too. Sometimes, inspiration begins with simple visibility—showing up, rising up, and staying up.

Pastor Dr. Claudine Benjamin

Zara never lectures Eli into flying. She lets her glide speak for her. Her poise under pressure, her rest in the wind, her trust in the unseen current—all of it inspires Eli to trust his own wings.

Your life becomes a message when:

- You remain faithful through transition.

- You pursue purpose with integrity.

- You get back up after falling.

- You soar with grace and humility.

Flight Insight: Don't hide your flight. Someone's breakthrough depends on your visibility.

MENTORING FROM THE SKY: TEACHING WITHOUT GROUNDING

Inspiration isn't about dragging others—it's about calling them higher. One of the greatest roles you can play in someone's journey is that of a midair mentor. Not one who waits until they are perfect to teach them, but one who speaks truth while they are still learning to flap.

Obed doesn't shame Eli for his wobbly starts. He shares his own stumbles, his crashes, his storms. His scars are his credentials. He reminds Eli: *"You don't inspire with perfection—you inspire with process."*

184

In Full Flight

Ways to inspire through mentorship:

- Tell your story, not just your success.
- Share your failures without shame.
- Offer guidance, not control.
- Be patient with their pace.

Flight Insight: Inspiration doesn't say, "Be like me." It says, "Be fully you."

HELPING OTHERS FACE THE NEST

Before any eagle can soar, it must first confront the comfort of the nest. The nest is warm. Familiar. Safe. But eventually, it becomes a cage. Your job in inspiring others is often to nudge—not push—those around you to face their potential over their preference for safety.

In Deuteronomy 32:11, Scripture paints the picture of an eagle stirring its nest—fluffing the comfort out so the eaglet learns to stretch its wings. Sometimes, the most loving thing you can do is disrupt someone's comfort so they can discover their capacity.

How to stir the nest in love:

- Ask hard questions that provoke growth.
- Challenge comfort-based mindsets.
- Encourage faith steps, not fear-based stagnation.
- Be present when they fall—but don't prevent the fall.

185

Pastor Dr. Claudine Benjamin

Flight Insight: Comfort never births courage. Stir the nest when it's time.

CREATING SKY CULTURE: WHEN EVERYONE FLIES HIGHER

When you inspire one person to fly, you create a ripple. But when you create an atmosphere of encouragement, empowerment, and accountability, you create sky culture—a spiritual environment where everyone is expected to rise.

This is the culture Zara and Obed intentionally cultivate. It's not competitive—it's collective. No one needs to outfly the other. Instead, they celebrate each other's elevation.

Signs of a sky culture:

- People cheer when others succeed.
- Accountability is not shaming but sharpening.
- Wings are strengthened, not clipped.
- There's a focus on destiny, not drama.

You have the power to shape the airspace around you. What kind of culture are you creating—on your team, in your ministry, in your family?

Flight Insight: Culture determines altitude. Build an atmosphere where soaring is normal.

SPARK THE FLIGHT, SHARE THE SKY

There's a reason the eagle doesn't stay in the nest alone. Flight is meant to be multiplied. Whether you're helping someone launch, navigate, rebuild, or trust the wind again, your obedience to soar can become their inspiration to rise.

Never underestimate your impact. Every time you rise, you show someone it's possible.

So flap louder. Glide stronger. Trust deeper. And as you do—look around. The sky is filling up. Because of your flight, someone else is learning to take off.

PRAYER

Father, let my life be a light that inspires others to rise. Use my journey to awaken the dreams of those around me. Let my testimony stir courage and ignite vision in the hearts of others who are called to soar.

Scripture: Matthew 5:16 – *"Let your light so shine before men, that they may see your good works, and glorify your Father which is in heaven."*

CHAPTER 23

LEAVING FLIGHT PATHS FOR FUTURE GENERATIONS

SOARING BEYOND SELF – BUILDING LEGACY IN THE SKY

The flight is not just about where you're going—it's about who's coming behind you.

In the natural world, mature eagles do something remarkable: they don't just fly to survive. They soar to instruct. They leave patterns, paths, and practices for the younger eagles watching from below. Though the sky is vast, they understand their role in shaping the next generation of fliers.

Spiritually, we are not only called to fly well—we are called to leave maps.

Our lives, choices, disciplines, and even our struggles all become landmarks for those who will rise after us. Legacy isn't only what you leave behind—it's what you leave above.

Pastor Dr. Claudine Benjamin

THE PURPOSE OF YOUR PATH

You may not realize it, but every time you obey God, you carve a flight path in the spirit. Every prayer you pray, every storm you overcome, every time you forgive, persist, worship, or trust in the face of fear—you're creating a spiritual air trail.

Someone will follow it.

You're showing your children, disciples, community, and even silent observers that soaring is possible. You are becoming living proof that God's grace can sustain, that His promises still come true, and that faith still lifts us above the noise.

Flight Insight: Your altitude creates access. Your obedience opens doors.

ELI'S FUTURE DEPENDS ON OBED'S LEGACY

In the world of your book, the seasoned eagle, Obed, doesn't just fly—he leaves markers. Every scar on his wings becomes a story. Every decision he makes influences Eli's journey. And Eli—though unsure and in training—will one day teach another because of what Obed imparted.

That's the power of generational flight: Your story becomes someone else's survival guide.

Obed's wisdom is not just words—it's direction. His legacy is more than memory—it's momentum.

Key Thought: Legacy isn't about being remembered. It's about building a path someone else can walk—or fly—on.

ZARA'S GRACE: MODELING FLIGHT WITH EXCELLENCE

Zara, the soaring eagle, leaves behind an atmosphere. She shows younger eagles not just how to fly but how to do it with grace. Her self-discipline, timing, reverence for the wind—these become imprints in the spiritual atmosphere that shape the culture of flight.

The generations watching her don't just want to fly—they want to fly well. They want to carry the same anointing, poise, and unwavering trust in God.

Legacy Truth: You don't inspire with perfection. You inspire by flying authentically with God.

BUILDING ALTARS IN THE SKY

In scripture, Abraham, Isaac, Jacob, and others built altars wherever they encountered God. These altars weren't just places of worship—they were memorials for future generations to remember what God did.

When you live a life of purpose and prayer, you're building altars in the sky. Future generations will fly by your faith decisions and recognize that *"this is a place where God met my mother, pastor, mentor, father... and He will meet me here too."*

—— Your consistency builds an altar.

Pastor Dr. Claudine Benjamin

— Your forgiveness builds an altar.
— Your sacrifices build altars.
— Your yes to God creates legacy.

Flight Insight: You are not just flying. You are marking the map.

PREPARING THE NEST, THEN PUSHING THEM OUT

Every eagle builds a nest for its young—but eventually, that nest must be stirred. In love, not cruelty, the eagle makes the environment uncomfortable to provoke the eaglet to fly.

Legacy isn't just about provision—it's about preparation.

Preparing the next generation to fly means:

- Giving them truth, not just comfort.
- Modeling spiritual disciplines they can replicate.
- Releasing control so they can learn to flap.
- Being present when they fall, but not preventing the fall.

You were never meant to keep others in the nest—you were meant to launch them.

Key Lesson: Legacy is not about keeping people close. It's about teaching them how to soar on their own.

THE SKY IS GENERATIONAL

God's sky isn't limited to your season. His purposes span generations. You are part of a divine timeline. You're not just flying for today—you're flying for tomorrow.

192

In Full Flight

— Your ceiling becomes their floor.
— Your altitude becomes their launching pad.
— Your faith creates space for their boldness.

And just as you followed the wind God provided, someone else is preparing to follow yours.

"One generation shall praise thy works to another, and shall declare thy mighty acts." **—Psalm 145:4**

YOUR FLIGHT IS A LEGACY IN MOTION

You are writing a legacy with every wingbeat. You are not flying alone—and you're not flying just for you. Every obedience, prayer, and act of courage is making the sky safer, clearer, and more accessible for those who will soar after you.

So keep flying.

Not just higher—but wiser. Not just stronger—but sacrificially. One day, when your wings are tired and your assignment is fulfilled, another eagle will take off from the place you left your final imprint.

— Let them fly farther.
— Let them fly free.
— Let them fly because you showed them it could be done.

Pastor Dr. Claudine Benjamin

PRAYER

God, help me to leave a legacy that others can follow. May the paths I blaze through faith, perseverance, and obedience become highways of destiny for future generations. Let my ceiling be their floor.

Scripture: Proverbs 13:22 – *"A good man leaveth an inheritance to his children's children: and the wealth of the sinner is laid up for the just."*

CHAPTER 24

LANDING IN PURPOSE

DESCENDING WITH DIRECTION – FULFILLING THE FLIGHT YOU WERE CALLED TO TAKE

Every flight, no matter how high or how long, must eventually land.

Eagles don't stay in the air forever. Pilots don't circle indefinitely. And believers weren't created just to fly aimlessly—we were created to land with intention, to arrive at the place God designed for our destiny. Soaring is powerful but landing in purpose is essential.

This chapter isn't about the thrill of takeoff or the strength of midair maintenance. It's about the sacred moment when God says, *"Now descend. Now deliver. Now dwell in what I've been preparing you for."*

WHAT DOES IT MEAN TO "LAND IN PURPOSE"?

To land in purpose means:

- You've moved from potential to fulfillment.

195

- You've shifted from running to rooting.
- You've recognized where God is planting you—and you stay.

It's the moment when:

- Your calling is no longer theory—it's practice.
- You stop questioning your worth and start walking in your assignment.
- You embrace the weight of destiny and release the pressure of performance.

"I have fought a good fight, I have finished my course, I have kept the faith:" —2 Timothy 4:7

Paul didn't say, "I flew high." He said, "I finished my course." That's purpose. That's legacy. That's landing well.

RECOGNIZING WHEN IT'S TIME TO LAND

Many of us love the thrill of starting. Few of us recognize when it's time to settle into the assignment. Landing isn't a downgrade—it's a deployment.

Here are signs you're entering your "landing in purpose" season:

- Clarity begins replacing curiosity.
- You feel called to commit more deeply, not float aimlessly.
- Your past seasons start to make sense in light of what you're stepping into.

- You stop chasing opportunity and start honoring responsibility.

God doesn't call you to just chase spiritual adrenaline—He calls you to carry kingdom responsibility.

Flight Insight: Landing doesn't mean stopping. It means serving on solid ground.

THE IMPORTANCE OF LANDING WITH PRECISION

Just as pilots need a clear runway, a specific angle, and a smooth approach to land safely—so do we.

You cannot land in purpose with:

- Unresolved baggage.
- Unhealed wounds.
- Unconfessed fear.
- Unsubmitted pride.

Landing requires humility and intention.

It's not enough to just "do ministry," "start a business," or "use your gift." Purpose demands:

- Alignment with God's will.
- Consistency in obedience.
- Willingness to be rooted, mentored, and accountable.

Pastor Dr. Claudine Benjamin

Eagles who try to land in the wrong terrain injure themselves. The same is true spiritually—your landing zone matters. God has a specific place, people, and assignment tied to your wings.

"The steps of a good man are ordered by the Lord: and he delighteth in his way." —Psalm 37:23

WHAT LANDING LOOKS LIKE IN REAL LIFE

Landing in purpose might mean:

- Accepting a leadership role you once avoided.
- Saying yes to a ministry that stretches you.
- Starting the nonprofit, church, school, or book God has been whispering to you about.
- Parenting, mentoring, or teaching in a way that pours legacy into others.
- Committing to build, plant, and stay where you once only visited.

It's not glamorous. Sometimes it's lonely. But it's deeply fulfilling.

You begin to realize:

- "This is what I was born for."
- "This is why I survived what I did."
- "This is where I grow others, not just myself."

PREPARING FOR THE LANDING

Before the eagle lands, it slows down. It descends intentionally. It watches its landing zone. Spiritually, we too must prepare to land.

In Full Flight

This may mean:

- Decluttering your schedule to focus on your assignment.
- Strengthening disciplines (prayer, study, worship).
- Seeking wise counsel and spiritual mentorship.
- Practicing rest so you don't crash into burnout.
- Letting go of ego so you can carry responsibility.

God isn't just calling you to high places—He's calling you to establish something on the earth. Legacy lives in landing.

Flight Insight: You didn't soar just to be seen. You soared so you could settle in what God called you to steward.

THE FLIGHT WAS ALWAYS ABOUT PURPOSE

— You've stretched your wings.
— You've risen above storms.
— You've followed the wind of the Holy Spirit.

Now, God says, *"Land. Establish. Build."*

This is not the end of your journey—it's the beginning of fruitfulness.

You are not being grounded—you are being planted.

— So land in your assignment with boldness.
— Land in your calling with confidence.
— Land in your purpose with peace.

Pastor Dr. Claudine Benjamin

Because everything that came before—the flapping, storms, stretching, solitude—was all preparing you for this.

Land well. Live purposefully. Soar in legacy.

PRAYER

Lord, I trust You with both the flight and the landing. When I arrive in the place You've prepared for me, let me recognize it and rejoice in it. Help me to land with grace, humility, and a deep sense of fulfillment in Your purpose.

Scripture: Philippians 1:6 – *"Being confident of this very thing, that he which hath begun a good work in you will perform it until the day of Jesus Christ:"*

CHAPTER 25

IDENTIFYING YOUR EAGLE TYPE

PERSONAL REFLECTION QUESTIONS

1. Which eagle type do you most identify with right now? Why?
   (Visionary, Warrior, Soaring, Teaching, Weathered, or Rebuilding)

1. Have you ever tried to fly in someone else's pattern? What was the result?

2. What strengths are unique to your eagle type? How can you begin embracing them more fully?

3. What "flight warning" spoke most to you? Why?

4. Who in your life represents another eagle type that complements yours? How can you better honor their role?

DECLARATIONS: SPEAK OVER YOUR WINGS

- I was created to soar in the sky designed for me.
- I embrace my eagle type and will not compare my flight to another.

201

Pastor Dr. Claudine Benjamin

- My strengths are valuable, my process is necessary, and my purpose is divine.
- Even in molting, I am still an eagle.
- I will trust God as the Wind beneath my wings and fly with focus, grace, and power.

CHARACTER SYMBOLISM: ELI, ZARA, AND OBED

ELI – THE REBUILDING EAGLE BECOMING A WARRIOR

- Young and full of potential, Eli is learning the value of identity, obedience, and resilience.

- He represents believers in transition—those just discovering their wings or recovering from past wounds.

- As he grows, his boldness shows signs of a future Warrior Eagle.

ZARA – THE SOARING EAGLE WITH VISIONARY WISDOM

- Calm, focused, and deeply in tune with divine rhythm, Zara is led by the wind of the Spirit.

- Her glide speaks of spiritual maturity and trust.

- She carries both the Soaring and Visionary eagle traits—clear insight and deep peace.

In Full Flight

OBED – THE WEATHERED AND TEACHING EAGLE

- Scarred by storms, seasoned by survival, Obed is a father figure of flight.

- He trains younger eagles, shares hard-earned wisdom, and understands the cost of elevation.

- Obed blends the Teaching and Weathered eagle roles with grace.

PRAYER

Father, reveal to me who I truly am in Your eyes. Help me understand the type of eagle I am and the specific strengths and gifts You've given me. Teach me to embrace my uniqueness and soar in the identity You designed.

Scripture: Romans 12:6 – _"Having then gifts differing according to the grace that is given to us, whether prophecy, let us prophesy according to the proportion of faith;"_

CONCLUSION

THE SKY IS STILL CALLING

You've come through the nest. You've flapped in frustration. You've weathered storms. You've ridden winds. You've trusted God in turbulence. You've learned to wait, rise, descend, discern—and through it all, you've discovered what it truly means to live **in full flight.**

But let this be your reminder: **this is not the end—it's only the beginning.**

The skies of purpose are vast, and your calling is far from finished. What God has placed inside you cannot be grounded by fear, failure, or fatigue. You were created to fly—not just once, not just occasionally—but *continually*. Purpose is not a destination; it is a way of life. It's a commitment to live every day aligned with God's design, empowered by His Spirit, and driven by eternal assignment.

— You are no longer the grounded one.
— You are no longer the overlooked one.
— You are no longer the unsure eaglet.
— You are the eagle who has learned to soar with intention and trust.

Pastor Dr. Claudine Benjamin

YOU'VE GAINED ALTITUDE, NOW STAY THERE

Flight isn't just about rising once—it's about maintaining your elevation. Your job now is to protect your altitude:

- Stay submitted to the Holy Spirit.
- Stay sharpened by the Word.
- Stay surrounded by the right people.
- Stay committed to the process.

Every new level will require renewed trust. Every season will carry its own winds. But what you've learned has made you stronger, wiser, and more prepared for the skies ahead.

You now understand the power of:

- Faith-fueled lift-offs.
- Holy Spirit navigation.
- Storm management.
- Consistent elevation.
- Obedient descents.
- Purposeful landings.

That is the anatomy of a soaring life. That is what it means to fly with kingdom purpose.

YOU'RE NOT FLYING JUST FOR YOU

As you continue to fly, remember: your flight leaves a trail.

Eli is watching. The younger generation is watching. Those who feel stuck in their own nests are watching. And they don't need perfection from you—they need proof that it's possible to live above fear, shame, doubt, delay, and distraction.

Be the eagle who points others to the Wind.

Let your life shout:

- "Yes, you can rise."
- "Yes, you can heal."
- "Yes, you can follow Jesus with your whole heart."
- "Yes, the storm is real—but so is the lift of the Holy Spirit."

Your wings are not for ego. They are for impact.

A FINAL CHARGE TO THE SOARING ONES

You've walked through each chapter. You've dug deep into your design. You've allowed truth to peel back layers of insecurity and fear. Now what?

Now you fly.

- Not just in inspiration—but in implementation.
- Not just in boldness—but in obedience.
- Not just for speed—but for direction.
- Not just for applause—but for assignment.
- Fly with eyes fixed on heaven.
- Fly with a heart full of fire.
- Fly with ears tuned to the Spirit.

Pastor Dr. Claudine Benjamin

— Fly with a spirit ready to pour into others.

Because this world needs you—your generation needs you. Your family, ministry, assignment—they are waiting for the fully awakened, spiritually aware, purpose-driven eagle *you've become.*

KEEP SOARING

— When the winds shift, keep soaring.
— When the storms rise, keep soaring.
— When you don't feel strong, keep soaring.
— When no one applauds, keep soaring.

You are not alone in the sky. The Spirit of God is with you, the wind is beneath you, and legacy is ahead of you.

— You were born for this.
— You were chosen for this.
— You were anointed to fly.

Now take your place in the sky—and never look back.

SOARING TO THE FINISH

"I have fought a good fight, I have finished my course, I have kept the faith." —2 Timothy 4:7

As we prepare to descend toward the final pages of this book, let us pause mid-flight—not to land prematurely, but to reflect, refocus, and refuel. You've come a long way, and the journey has not been easy. From learning how to take off in purpose, to navigating the altitude of calling, facing the turbulence of trials, and responding to unexpected disturbances, you've embraced what it truly means to live life in full flight.

But more than a metaphor or concept, this has been a spiritual blueprint—an invitation to live with intentional altitude; a call to rise above distractions, delays, and discouragement—and to soar with the purpose and power God placed within you.

YOU WERE BORN TO FLY

You were never created to live grounded by fear, shame, or uncertainty. Like the eagle—one of God's most majestic creations—you were designed to stretch your wings, embrace the wind, and rise above the storm. You were born to live with vision, to fly with focus, and to lead with faith.

The enemy works tirelessly to keep you on the ground. Life tries to clip your wings with disappointment, betrayal, anxiety, and fatigue. But God says, *"they that wait upon the Lord shall renew their strength; they shall mount up with wings as eagles; they shall run, and not be weary; and they shall walk, and not faint."* **—Isaiah 40:31**

You're not just flying to escape your past—you're flying toward divine destiny.

WHAT YOU'VE GAINED IN THE FLIGHT

Throughout this book, you have learned that flying high isn't just about altitude—it's about attitude. You've gained:

- Faith that lifts you beyond fear.

Pastor Dr. Claudine Benjamin

- The Word that fuels you when the journey gets long.
- The Holy Spirit that empowers and sustains your flight.
- Obedience that steers you toward your assignment.
- Perseverance that keeps you in the air even during the longest battles.

You've learned that disturbances are not signs of failure but invitations to deeper trust. That storms don't cancel your destination—they often clarify it. That sudden shifts in direction doesn't mean God changed His mind—they mean He's preparing you for more than you expected.

THE LEGACY OF FLIGHT

When an eagle soars, it doesn't only fly for itself—it sets an example for the young. It leaves a trail in the sky for the next generation to follow. The same is true for you. Your flight is your legacy.

You are teaching others how to:

- Get up again after a crash.
- Fly with purpose through pain.
- Navigate spiritual airspace with courage.
- Land in purpose and rise again when called.

Whether you're Eli, the Young Eagle, still discovering the winds of destiny, Zara, the Soaring Eagle, seasoned and strong in your faith or Obed, the Weathered Eagle, carrying the wisdom of every storm you've survived, you are flying in purpose, and your story is still being written in the skies of eternity.

210

FINAL INSTRUCTIONS FROM THE TOWER

As every flight draws near its conclusion, the voice from the tower gives final instructions. So too, as you reach the end of this part of your journey, the voice of the Lord is speaking—not to land you, but to send you.

— You've been equipped.
— You've been elevated.
— You've been anointed to fly.

But now, it's time to apply what you've learned.

PRAYER

Lord, thank You for every lesson, every moment of growth, and every revelation shared through this journey. May these words take root and bear fruit in the lives of those who read them. Let every reader rise with wings like eagles, soaring into the fullness of their purpose in You. In Jesus' name. Amen.

Scripture: Isaiah 40:31 – *"But those who trust in the Lord will find new strength. They will soar high on wings like eagles. They will run and not grow weary. They will walk and not faint." - NLT*

Made in the USA
Middletown, DE
20 May 2025

75798396R00119